Basic Guide
to the
American Cocker Spaniel

*Written by breeders
who know the breed...
For those who are interested in
learning more about the
American Cocker Spaniel*

Published by Dace Publishing
P.O. Box 91, Ruckersville, VA 22968
To all those who have challenged me: "Here's to you....."

Printed in the United States of America

ISBN 0-932045-07-3
Library of Congress Catalog Card Number 94-72578

First Edition, 1996

Front Cover:
Ch. Regal's Tribute To Matador
owned by Pat & Betty Peck, Regal Cockers,
Long Beach, MS   See Page 64

Back Cover:
Ch. Cashmere's Amazing Grace,
owned by Debbie Bertrand & John Zolezzi,
Eighty-Eights, Fresno, TX
Bred and Co-owned by Lynn McLoughlin
See Page 64

The *Basic Guide to the American Cocker Spaniel* is written from information about the breed collected from some of the top breeders in the nation. Without their help, we could not truly reflect the breed and present it as unique within the world of dogs. We would like to thank the following people for their help in putting this project together.

Michael R. Zervas - Managing Editor
Stephen W. Jones - Project Editor
Sam Dickinson & Sylvia Keilitz - Project Co-Ordinators

And a special thank you for the tremendous help we received from the following owners, breeders and of course, lovers of the American Cocker Spaniel.

CONTRIBUTING AUTHORITIES IN NO PARTICULAR ORDER:

Jean Nelson	Jeff L. Wright	Mary Ann Meekins
Jim & Glenda Thorn	Herbert Kozuma	Linda Beatie
Dr. Colin Hagan	Dr. Swift	Becki & Dale Zaborowski
Alice Horton	Debbie Bertrand	Mary Galton
Michael Allen	Anne & T. W. Coleman	Joan & Tony Stallard
Brenda Hamm	John Zolezzi	Nancy & Tom Gallant
Cindy Lane	Maddie Brown	Connie & Jim Walsh
Leslie & Paul Weston	Tom & Dottie McCoy	Jack & Carolanne Garlick
Janet Little	Julie Kallbacka	Muriel Barber
Mary Stacey	Eileen Chenevert	Margaret McRae
Evelyn Bravo	Linda Donaldson	Jerry & Laurie Ables
Betty Willroth	Pat & Betty Peck	Dr Dennis & Roxanne Harris-Parks
Lynn McLoughlin	Laun Presser	

Your years of knowledge and interest in the breed, has not only made this book possible, but insures the future of the American Cocker Spaniel.

HOW TO USE THE BASIC GUIDE BREED SERIES

This series of books is written for the person who is investigating the breed for a possible pet; for the person who has decided on an American Cocker Spaniel and wants to know how to find a good breeder and what to ask; for the person who has just bought an American Cocker Spaniel who wants to know what to expect and how to train it; and for the person who owns an American Cocker Spaniel who wants to know more about the breed and how closely his or her dog resembles current champions of the breed. These books are also a *beginning point* for those who want to know what else they can do with their dogs in field work, showing, agility or breeding.

The Basic Guide to the American Cocker Spaniel takes a unique approach. Instead of being the opinion of one kennel, with one style of dog and one view of the breed, we have interviewed many breeders and have pooled their vast knowledge and interest in the breed to create an overview as **NO OTHER BREED BOOK** provides. The knowledge and experience reflected here are not limited to a single person.

This series is truly educational for the reader. In many places, where breeders have given us conflicting information, we have pooled that information, making note that there is dispute within the breed and indicating that further discussion with individual breeders is advisable.

OUR TWO SPECIAL SECTIONS

The **HALL OF FAME** section not only puts new people in contact with breeders of top quality animals as a place to start their search, but it also gives the reader a chance to see the different styles within the breed. By carefully studying the pedigrees provided, it is a start in understanding the relation of the pedigree to the individual dog - the cornerstone upon which breeds and breed registries are built. If you already own an American Cocker Spaniel, you might enjoy looking through this section and comparing your dog and its pedigree with those who have been achievers in the world of dogs!

Finally, the **SHOPPING ARCADE** section puts readers in contact with some of the fine businesses whose products relate to dogs and to American Cocker Spaniels in particular. For those of us who show dogs on a regular basis, we meet some of these fine specialty businesses every week. For those who do not attend such events, the Shopping Arcade section provides them a chance to find these quality products which will make excellent gifts for the breed lover, additions to your home, or products to help you raise a happy, healthy dog.

We sincerely hope you find this book informative and entertaining and that you have as much fun reading it as we have had producing it, and as much fun as our breeders have had producing fine quality dogs for so many years.

BEFORE YOU BUY A DOG

1) Decide WHAT YOU WANT THE DOG TO DO. Evaluate your home and lifestyle and how a dog should fit into your life.

2) Look at different breeds and decide what breed is best for you and your home.

3) Realize that there are differences in style and temperament within each breed. Different breeders select their breeding stock based on different criteria. Use the Hall of Fame to help you see the differences among dogs and kennels.

4) Find a breeder who produces dogs which will fit your needs. Ask questions which will insure that the dog you buy will be right for you by finding a breeder who places importance on the qualities which are important to you.

5) Be sure to ask the breeder the right questions for that particular breed and be prepared for what the breeder will want to ask you.

With this in mind, your decision will be an informed one and the dog you buy will be a welcome addition to your family for years to come.

Table of Contents

Ch. Shalimar's Regal Challenge, CDX, going over a jump in an obedience class. This winning American Cocker Spaniel was lovely enough to win his conformation championship, and talented enough to win his CDX title in the performance ring. As a companion, a lovely contestant in the show ring, or in obedience, agility or even frisbee competition, American Cocker Spaniels prove why the breed has become so popular around the world.

INTRODUCTION

We are often asked, "Why buy a purebred dog?" Certainly there are some wonderful, loving and even talented mutts. But have you ever owned a dog, or known a mutt you admired and been frustrated in trying to locate another like him?

Centuries ago, people kept dogs for pets, for working partners in their fields and with their flocks, as hunting companions, and for protection of the family. As dogs began to diversify, people noticed certain dogs were better at one thing than others. People liked the looks of one dog over another, or found that one had better instincts in certain areas than another. Dogs in one geographic area began to look alike from interbreeding within a small population, and people who lived in other areas came to buy such dogs when they wanted a certain characteristic or look. Thus dog breeds began to evolve. The breeds were based on predictability of looks and performance in a dog from a certain area or gene pool.

Breeders, and later field or kennel clubs began to keep records of individuals. This recording of the gene pool is a second step in creating a breed. Without such record keeping, a breed will change and lose characteristics. Again, it is insurance that a puppy will grow to look and act like certain other individuals.

Finally, people wrote descriptions of the breed. At first these were simply descriptions of certain dogs which impressed the author on a hunt, or in traveling. These descriptions are our earliest written standards. Later, breeders banded together to form breed clubs and they wrote a detailed, collective description of the breed for others to follow. Careful breeders who studied the standard, thought about the original purpose of the breed, and were concerned about health and temperament, continued the breed.

The value of a breed, and a registration to record it, is that a buyer of a puppy can predict what it will look like when it is grown up, what the talents will be, what the temperament will be like and how well it will fit a living situation. If we owned and raised nothing but crossbreeds, or if you simply got a cute puppy from the dog pound, you would have no way of knowing what you might be sharing your home and your life with for the next twelve to fourteen years!

And there is a certain pride of ownership in a stylish, quality dog. It does not take an experienced eye to tell the difference between a fine antique and a fake, between a fine luxury car and a clunker. To say that there is no reason to get a purebred dog instead of a mutt is like saying that a Geo will get you there just as well as a Cadillac. Both fill the same job of taking the driver from one place to another, but the pride of ownership is entirely different. It does not take training to recognize quality in an animal. It is manifested in the way the dog comes together, the way the over-all animal pleases the eye, the attitude and presence — self confidence — of the dog. Good breeding, soundness, and aptitude of purpose are a source of pleasure. If *you divide the cost of the average puppy from a good breeder, by the life span of the dog, you will be paying less than $50.00 a year, or about $4.00 a month for the pleasure of an animal that will be recognizable as his breed, serve the purpose for which he was bred, and have the health and temperament that will make him fit your family and life-style.*

In this way, you will find an animal that will be a good fit, one that will share your home and your love for a lifetime, instead of getting a puppy that grows into an individual you cannot live with, and one which causes frustration and stress.

Breeders find that new owners who take this kind of time to locate a puppy are far more likely to be satisfied with their new family member. They are more likely to realize what care of that breed will entail, will be more likely to provide a long-term, good home, and far less likely to take it to the pound or otherwise get rid of the animal.

So, take the time to do your homework about the breed. A dog is not only what it looks like, but how easy it is to live with in a given situation. No breed is perfect for everyone. Find out what questions to ask for that particular breed, locate breeders, and take your time to find a puppy or adult dog which will meet your needs. For those purposes, we hope these <u>BASIC GUIDE</u> *books will be helpful.*

HISTORY

Spaniels have been in the history of dogs since the early 1300's, although dogs with a resemblance to Spaniels date back to ancient times. The word "Spaniel" comes from Spain, designating a dog from that country. The first mention in English literature comes in the 1340's when Chaucer wrote "For as a Spanyel she wol on him lepe" in *Prologue to Wyf of Bathe's Tales.*

In 1387 the French Count Gaston de Foix indicated that the Spaniel was well known in his part of France, which was close to Spain. The Count was a good hunter and very interested in dogs. He wrote of the nature of Spaniels, their good points and their bad. He described them as devoted to their masters, wagging their tails in happy pursuit of partridge and quail. But, he cautioned, they were fighters and barkers and would often lead the greyhounds astray.

The Count's writing was translated into English by the Duke of York in 1410. Edward, the second Duke of York, wrote of the breed as "Hounds of the Hawk." There are breeders who believe that although named "Spaniels," the breed might not have come from Spain, and several other countries have been cited. The Duke of York's writings have been used to support both sides of this issue. In any case, Edward noted that "like the country that they came from," they had bad qualities. He said they barked a lot and were often wild and a nuisance. Some of our breeders noted that the dog today has many of the same qualities, and it is through understanding the Cocker, his origins and his bloodlines, that a good dog, solid in temperament, is found.

Wherever the breed originated, it is easy to say that during the thirteenth and fourteenth centuries, before huntsmen used guns in the field, falcons were used by wealthy sportsmen. These birds were sent aloft where they circled, keeping the game in cover of bush. The Spaniel scented out the location of the game, went down to it, and crept close, getting the attention of the game. The hunters would place a net over the dog and game alike. When necessary, Spaniels could swim and dive under water to retrieve wounded game.

Early on, Spaniels were divided into two varieties, land and water. All of the Spaniel breeds have evolved from those early divisions. Even Setters have evolved from the crossing of the Spanish Pointer with the Spaniel. This cross took place after the gun displaced the falcon and net in sport hunting around 1775. Early guns took a long time to load and aim. If the game moved, hunters were unable to shoot and hit it. The lively Spaniel was a nuisance, frightening the birds and rabbits. The smaller, quiet lap dog varieties became more popular. Some terms used to describe early Spaniel breeds were Springer, Springing Spaniel, Cocker, Cocking Spaniel and Cock Flusher. One trait that shows in all of the Spaniel breeds are the long ears. Early drawings by an Italian naturalist in the fifteenth century show the long, floppy ears.

Spaniels are mentioned in a rare work called Boke of St. Albans, attributed to a nun called Dame Julia Berners, and are shown in the courtly paintings of the English nobility. King Henry VIII is said to have paid five shillings for the return of a lost Spaniel of which he was especially fond. The courts of several nobles showed records of expenses for Spaniel keepers and the cloth they used to rub the dogs' coats.

By 1837, the English Spaniel had been developed into a breed and this change became apparent as new classes were introduced at shows. Shorter legged Cockers and longer legged Springers also began to evolve. In the Birmingham show in 1859, for the first time a class was given for "Spaniels, Cocker." This was a sporting dog show, and by 1860 Cockers were no longer a breed but were simply a different size classification of Spaniels. Large size and small size Spaniel classes allowed Cockers to compete in the small size class.

Cockers found their way to America in the late nineteenth century. They were characterized as Cockers, but not yet recognized as an entirely separate breed. They were separated by size from Field Spaniels. If the dog was under twenty-eight pounds it was entered as a Cocker. Larger than that, it was a Field Spaniel. This meant both Cocker Spaniels and Field Spaniels could come from the same litter. In 1901 the American Spaniel Club abolished this definition by size and more uniformity of type was immediately noticeable. Progress of the Cocker Spaniel as a breed has moved forward ever since.

The first line of Cockers to become recognized was the Obo Kennel of Mr. James Farrow of England. The original Obo was whelped in June 14, 1879. His sire, Fred, and his dam, Betty, were both descendants of Mr. Burdett's Spaniels. Through line breeding of Obo, Mr. Farrow developed consistent style and type. He exhibited his dogs frequently and kept careful pedigree records. Ch. Obo was shown for eight years and never defeated in classes provided for Cocker Spaniels. Most of today's good black lines of Cockers extend back to Obo.

Chloe II was bred to Obo and imported to America in whelp. One of her pups, Obo II, was sold as a small black puppy to Mr. J.P. Wiley of Salmon Falls, New Hampshire, who registered him as Obo II AKC No 4911. He began to show in 1883, and he won Best Cocker owned by a Spaniel Club member at Madison Square Garden that year. This was before AKC was recognized in 1884, but after the American Spaniel Club was founded in 1881. (Madison Square Garden, which was first held in 1877, is the second oldest continuous sporting event in the United States behind the Kentucky Derby, which was first held in 1875.) Two separate and distinct types of Cockers began to emerge about that time. The English Cocker began to diverge from the American version, which has a shorter, cobbier body, more profuse coat and a heavier, shorter head.

During the last part of the 1800's, many parti-colors were bred, mostly liver and whites and black and tans. By 1875, black and tans had become very popular. When the AKC began to divide Cocker Spaniels into color varieties, Mr. Payne of Midkiff Kennels in Kingston, Pennsylvania, became the leading breeder of parti-colored show Cockers. Ch.

Blue Bells II was a lovely bitch owned and shown by Mr. Payne who made a big impression on the parti-colored Cockers in this country.

By 1920 the popularity of the Cocker was growing by leaps and bounds. Again, Mr. Payne's kennel was at the forefront with the 1921 Westminster Kennel Club winner. Specialty clubs were being formed and the American Spaniel Club began holding its annual specialty show in January. That show is still going on today and many of our Hall of Fame dogs note their wins at that famous show. Although the show is open to all Spaniels, the American Cocker usually accounts for the most entries and most of the top winners.

Although the English type and the American type began to take shape from the early years of breeding, it was not until 1946 that the AKC actually granted recognition of the two separate Cocker breeds. Up to that time, the winners of the two color varieties of American Cockers and the winner of the "English-type" would compete for the "Best Cocker Spaniel" and only the winner of that award was eligible to go back for the group competition.

The American Cocker Spaniel rapidly rose to become the single most popular breed in America's history. For most of the years since WWII the American Cocker Spaniel has been in the top ten most popular breeds; many of those years have found it number one. In 1993 American Cocker Spaniels were number four and in 1994 the breed was number six.

In the 1930's the AKC divided the Cocker Spaniel into two completely separate color varieties for the purposes of showing: solid and parti-colored. Solid colors were further divided into classes for black and solids other than black. Black and tan dogs were originally shown in the parti-colored classes, but they are from black litters and were eventually moved into the black classes. During the 1940's the black dominated the show ring, but today, Best in Show winners come from all color varieties.

AMERICAN COCKERS IN OTHER COUNTRIES

Although originally the product of America, the American Cocker Spaniel has become a worldwide favorite. Beginning shortly after WWII, the American Cocker Spaniel gained popularity all over the world. Although every country began with American stock, Cockers bred from many generations of stock outside this country are winning throughout the world. Breeders such as Bea Wegusen exhibited their best stock in Mexico and Canada and introduced an appreciation of good Cockers in judges and breeders alike in those countries. Canada and Mexico have imported a number of American Cockers and have developed a number of very nice lines on their own. Cuba had a number of good breeders and the breed was very popular before the Communist regime took power and discouraged all dog breeding.

The United Kingdom has become very devoted to the American Cocker Spaniel in spite of the fact that this breed sprang from the English Cocker only a relatively short time ago. Many American Cockers of great fame have shown and won at the most prestigious shows in Britain. In fact, in spite of severe quarantine restrictions which apply to dogs being imported to the U.K., a number of breeders have taken the time, trouble and money to begin breeding programs in England, New Zealand and even Australia.

On the continent, American Cocker Spaniels have won both field and show titles. Holland, Sweden and Germany are but a few of the countries with a growing number of Cockers. Beginning in the late 1960's and early 1970's, this breed grew in popularity and a number of good breeders have emerged.

Cockers are well represented in South America with Brazil having a very active interest. Some of their most famous handlers make regular trips to the United States. There have been a number of American breeders who have sent good show stock into South American countries to be shown. You will see that some of the dogs in our Hall of Fame section hold championship titles in more than one country, including several South American countries.

One reason why the American Cocker Spaniel has spread all over the world is that the Cocker is small enough to ship easily by air and he loves to travel.

In recent years, since the breakup of the Communist regime in Russia, a number of Cockers have been exported to begin breeding programs in the former USSR. The breed now ranks in the top three most popular breeds of registered dogs in that country!

The Philippines have taken a large number of Cockers for show and breeding and Japan has produced some lovely dogs with foundations from some of the top kennels in America. The Japan Cocker Spaniel Association was founded in 1964 and flourishes with many enthusiastic owners and good breeders.

The American Cocker Spaniel has truly become an ambassador for the United States around the world. Popular the world over, the American Cocker Spaniel is the only dog breed of American origin in the AKC top twenty, and far and away the most popular American breed the world over.

SHOULD YOU BUY AN AMERICAN COCKER SPANIEL?

Like many popular breeds, a proliferation of "back yard breeders" and "pet shop breeders" have made an impression on the American Cocker Spaniel. Any time a breed becomes very popular, and therefore easy to sell, breeders who are not as dedicated to preserving the breed characteristics as much as they are interested in obtaining AKC papers and making a profit, tend to enter the market . It is therefore VERY important in terms of the dog's quality, temperament and style that you buy from a reputable breeder.

Cockers have become known as "excitable," and "yappy." Some have gotten the bad reputation of being snappy with children and difficult to housetrain. Although there are a great many dogs bearing registration papers which do indeed have these qualities, the Cockers should be "busy," but not yappy, active more than excitable. Cockers which are well bred are trainable and are solid family pets. The difference between poor quality dogs which are not well bred and those which have been bred by responsible breeders is a world apart.

Before buying a puppy, consider if you are really ready to buy a dog and then make a few basic decisions. Dogs, unlike fish or plants, take a commitment of time, energy and money beyond the initial purchase and the act of feeding and watering. A dog needs regular veterinary care, shots every year, time to be socialized and trained, time to be a companion and, with the Cocker and other long haired breeds, time to be groomed. They also need equipment like crates, beds, collars and toys to keep them occupied. As we have

mentioned, Cockers are very trainable, but an untrained Cocker, like many other breeds, is an effort to tolerate and difficult to enjoy.

Throughout this book, you will see the breed referred to as "American Cocker Spaniel." Even where we simply say "Cocker Spaniel," we are referring to the American Cocker. Generally, "Cocker Spaniel," "American Cocker" and "American Cocker Spaniel," all refer to the same, popular breed. Most of the Cockers you see or hear about will be American Cockers since they far outnumber their English counterpart. But be aware that there is also a separate breed called the "English Cocker Spaniel." There is some confusion in the minds of pet owners as to the difference. As we discussed in the history chapter, these spaniels were originally not broken apart as different breeds, but evolved into different breeds as the years went on. Today the English Cocker looks very different from the American Cocker. American Cockers have larger eyes, shorter heads, are shorter in leg, and carry a fuller show coat than their English cousins. The

English Cocker is calmer and is frequently seen in roan, a color which is not frequent in the American Cocker Spaniel. If you are interested in the difference, going to a dog show may be a good idea. Once you see the two breeds in person, it will be easy for you to tell the difference. To get a quick idea of how the two breeds look different, turn to page 76. The logo at the bottom of the page has an American Cocker Spaniel on the left, and an English Cocker Spaniel on the right.

Evaluate your home. How much room do you have for the dog? Do you have a fenced yard? Who will take care of the dog on a daily basis? How much time to you have to socialize it, and can you train a puppy? What do you want the dog to do? Will he be a companion which travels with you? Will there be children who come in on a regular basis or do you have children? Are you expecting to start a family within the lifetime of the dog? Will the dog live with other pets or other dogs? Does everyone in the family want the dog, or just one or two people?

Cockers are a good size for a small house. They can join in with a family and are good travelers if they are acclimatized early. They are energetic and like to play. They are active enough to join in exercise such as biking or jogging, and they will go through the fields with great abandon, enjoying the great outdoors. They like water and can be trained as good field dogs with the right bloodline and some patient training.

The Cocker Spaniel is a darling looking animal with large, kind eyes and the warmth of a teddy bear. But this loving, playful bundle of energy and mischief is not for everyone. Boundless energy and an interest in everything from the inside of cupboards to the bottom of the flowerbed make the Cocker a challenge to live with without regular training. His enthusiasm for anything which catches his attention and his natural happy temperament sometimes make him slow to learn a lesson which is not of particular interest to him.

Cockers are not stupid, but things often catch their attention to the point of distraction from what they should be learning. One of our breeders reported selling a Cocker to a family which lived out in a rural area with cattle. The dog loved to run through the fields with the cattle and was undeterred by an electric fence which was so low that he hit his back every time he went under it and got an electric shock. Instead of staying out of the pasture, he would become so intent on the fun he had with the cattle, he would forget about the fence and the discomfort it caused him. Another breeder suggested it was not that the American Cocker did not want to please; he is very interested in pleasing his master and seeks approval. But he is interested in so many things that he finds it difficult to concentrate when there is activity around him.

The American Cocker is not low maintenance. He requires attention from his master, is almost always interested in whatever his humans are doing, and needs both grooming and bathing on a regular basis. He needs firm, gentle discipline, as he will get his feelings hurt easily and can easily suffer from a heavy hand. If you are looking for a dog who can spend time alone, and leave you alone, the Cocker is not the breed for you. Instead of minding his own business, the Cocker is almost constantly interested in minding yours!

He is protective of his family, and loves to play. He will live to be twelve to fifteen years of age, often getting along fine even

after he is blind or deaf from old age. The sense of smell is strong, and in familiar circumstances he can still lead a happy, comfortable life.

The American Cocker Spaniel has soulful eyes and an appealing look. As a puppy, he has a look which will take your heart away. He has a loving, playful personality, but he requires daily attention. The American Cocker you purchase will need ample daily doses of love, attention, consistent discipline that is firm but NOT severe and abusive, and enough exercise to allow his energy to find an outlet. Although the American Cocker Spaniel will be happy to stay home while the family is at school or at work, once someone arrives home he does not want to spend time alone while the family or master go about their business. The Cocker will want to know what everyone is doing all the time and will often want to help them do it!

Don't forget, the Cocker will need to be groomed on a regular basis. Famous dogs in our Hall of Fame section are presented in show coat, which takes hours of grooming and care. You will probably keep your dog in a pet clip but you will need to plan for regular care of the coat, either by sending your dog to the groomer or by keeping him groomed and clipped at home. The coat tangles easily, and once mats begin, they are difficult to remove without cutting them out. If you intend to keep your Cocker shaved down completely so he does not need grooming, you are better off getting a dog with a short, smooth coat for easy maintenance, instead of one whose charm involves his lovely, flowing coat. These decisions need to be considered when you evaluate the Cocker to decide if it is the right breed for you and your home.

Find out what the breed is like from talking to several breeders. Ask about factors which are important to you and your situation. Each year, hundreds and thousands of lovely, purebred dogs end up at the SPCA, and people who have invested money in a good dog are discouraged to find that the pet they dreamed would become a part of their lives for years to come, has become a nightmare. Not EVERY dog in the breed will be the same and not EVERY home is the same. What will fit for one family will be a disaster in another. People have different life patterns, and different lifestyles, not to mention differences in homes, yards and time commitments. And people are attracted to different personalities in dogs. What may be fun and appealing to one person may be tiresome and destructive to another. It is important that you begin the process of looking for a dog by carefully evaluating what you want the dog to do, how you want it to behave, and how you want it to live.

Within each breed, there will be conflicting views. Most breeders will tell you that their breed is the best. If they didn't think so, they would be putting their time and energy into a different breed. Sometimes dog breeders raise or show several breeds before settling on the one to which they will dedicate their lives and fortunes! But different breeds have TENDENCIES toward certain characteristics based on their history, temperament, size and physical limitations or attributes.

For example, Cockers were originally field dogs. They love the water and will head for water or mud in the yard instead of avoiding it. This is not always the thing that makes the owner happy when he finds the sprinklers dug up, the flowers rearranged, and the lovely

Cocker coat caked in mud. None of this will make any difference to the Cocker, who thinks he should come in the house when he is finished playing and will not even notice his coat is less than pristine! The field dog instinct makes him playful, active, and willing to play ball and fetch. The same retrieving instinct that makes him run after a ball and bring it back also compels him to carry shoes and toys from room to room, depositing them when something else takes his eye.

Most dogs who end up in the SPCA are there not because they are BAD dogs, but because they did not fit their homes. Think about it as if you wanted a sports car, but had five children to carry around! It wouldn't be very long before the sports car was up for sale. But it would not be because sports cars are not fun, or because it did not perform well. It simply could not do the job that the family with five children needed it to do; it did not fit the situation or the home of the driver.

Another reason dogs end up in the SPCA is that their owners have underestimated the time it takes to socialize and train a puppy. Active breeds with an enthusiastic outlook on life need exercise and training. Without those two things, the dog will be excitable and uncontrollable. Training sessions do not have to be long, but they need to be frequent and consistent. Be sure you have the time to devote and a place for exercise before you buy a Cocker Spaniel.

Once you have determined what you intend to do with the dog, and that the Cocker Spaniel is right for your home, contact several breeders. They will be able to give you a detailed idea of how they see the breed. Ask them about specific situations which you feel will be typical of your lifestyle and living conditions and see if they feel the breed — and their dogs — will do well in those circumstances. These questions about specific situations will help you determine if the breed is right for you, instead of asking general questions about the breed and hearing a breeder's glowing report about why he likes the breed. *Assume that by virtue of the fact that he is breeding Cockers, the breeder is dedicated and loves the Cocker Spaniel. But you need to establish some way to measure if the breed will be RIGHT FOR YOU.* No single breed is perfect for everyone. We breed and buy purebred dogs so that there is some predictability of what the puppy will be like. Use that predictability to determine if you will be happy with the pup or older dog BEFORE you buy. You will be happier, the match between owner and dog will be better, and it will make for a happier life for everyone concerned and prevent good dogs from ending up in animal shelters.

One of our breeders said, "I am annoyed when people spend more time looking into the qualities of a T.V. set or computer than they do into a dog. The dog will come into their homes and be part of their lives for more years than either appliance will last!"

Ask your breeder about the standard, and how his dogs match and where they deviate. A standard is very important to breeders because it gives them something written against which to measure their dogs. Without a written standard, a breed would change freely at the whim of what was popular with judges and fanciers at the time. The standard pulls the breed back to the middle of the range, but individual dogs will vary in some ways. In fact, there is seldom a dog who matches the standard perfectly. Breeding with the standard in mind is one thing that marks the difference between good breeders and "puppy mills," or uneducated "backyard breeders." Breeders who take the time and trouble to learn their breed, to evaluate their dogs, and to make breeding which will keep their puppies in the range where they are good representatives of their breed are those who best ensure the future of the American Cocker Spaniel. These breeders are best able to predict what a puppy will grow up to be, if he will represent his breed in conformation and temperament, and if you will be pleased to spend years of your life with him.

Many pet owners ask why it should make any difference to them if a breeder breeds to the standard. The reason is quite obvious. If, as a new owner, you have taken the time to look into the breed, to select a style which fits your family and your needs, and one whose appearance is pleasing to you, and you purchase a puppy based on that decision, you have a right to a dog which will grow up and be recognizable as that breed. To buy a dog

from less than a reputable breeder is like being satisfied in driving a new car with a lot of dents just because the dealer could sell you a particular model for a lower price. As long as a dog has AKC papers, and he is bred to a bitch with AKC papers and the paperwork is in order, AKC will issue papers for the puppies. But that does not ensure that those puppies will indeed grow up to be representative of their breed. For

that, you must trust your breeder. Generations of breeding without regard to the standard will produce puppies which, at best, are barely recognizable as the breed.

If you already own a Cocker, look at the photos in the Hall of Fame section and see how your dog compares. When buying a dog, look at the parents if possible and compare them to the Hall of Fame dogs.

There are dozens of dogs in the animal shelter. Why pay even a few hundred dollars for a purebred dog and still have to answer the question, "What kind of dog is that?" Predictability of what you will have when the dog grows up, pride in ownership, the joy of having a fine looking dog, is similar to having a quality car instead of simply transportation!

When you have decided that the American Cocker Spaniel is the dog for you, there are several ways to locate a puppy or older dog. Many pet shops have Cockers. They are very popular and the Cocker is a "puppy" breed. By that, we mean that some breeds are very cute as puppies and very appealing to the buyer. These are the kinds of breeds pet shops like because pet shop buying of a puppy is often an impulse. You see a cute puppy in the window or in the cage and decide at that point that you want a new dog. This is the type of purchase which most frequently ends up with a mismatch between the dog and the home, and the owner may later decide to drop the dog off at the SPCA or give him away.

Reputable breeders will not sell their puppies to pet shops. They are able to sell their puppies to good homes and they do not produce more puppies than they are able to sell. Most pet shops buy their pups from "puppy mills," which breed any dog with papers to any bitch with papers without regard to the quality of the dog or how representative it may be for its breed. These puppies are often raised in cages and moved as a litter to wholesalers, then shipped to the retailer at a very early age. They seldom have the kind of early puppy socialization and handling that those from a breeder will have experienced, and consequently they are more likely to have temperaments which are excitable, destructive or defensive. Pet shop prices will be as high or higher than the prices from a reputable breeder, so it makes more sense to seek out a breeder and use your money to buy a good dog which will bring you years of happiness and joy.

Another avenue is to buy a puppy from the newspaper. Since you must find the newspaper and look for a breeder, you have at least had time to think about whether you really want a puppy. You can call and see what they have available and make a trip to the breeder's home. Reputable breeders sometimes sell their pups through the newspaper, but the vast majority of newspaper ads will be from "backyard" breeders. These people have

often simply bred their bitch to any local stud. They have no idea of the breeding behind their dogs, what kinds of health problems may be lurking in the pedigree ready to affect the puppies, or how to match traits of the parents in order to ensure that the puppies are of good quality. These puppies are cheap, but they usually do not carry any health guarantee. Even in states which require the breeder to be responsible for the puppy's health, these backyard breeders are exempted because they do not produce more than one or two litters a year. You can end up spending more money than you save on vet costs and may still not end up with a dog which is a good specimen of a Cocker Spaniel. Many breed clubs advise people that the WORST first step is to go and look at a litter of puppies from the local newspaper. The chances are you will fall in love with the adorable pups and your heart can easily overrule your head.

In short, a pet shop will be expensive for the quality you receive, but there will be a health guarantee of some kind. A backyard breeder will usually not have any kind of guarantee, and the pups may be of mixed quality in terms of health and conformation. Take your time and look for a reputable breeder. You may pay about what you will pay for the pet shop puppy, but you will get not only a guarantee, but a good representation of a Cocker Spaniel and you will have some idea about the style and temperament of the puppy before you buy.

TAKE YOUR TIME AND DO YOUR HOMEWORK. This will ensure that you end up with a dog which will be a good companion for many years to come. It is important to buy from a reputable breeder in all breeds, but American Cocker Spaniels are one of the breeds where it is particularly important. Careful, knowledgeable breeders can provide you with a puppy which has all the traits and temperament qualities which brought this breed to the forefront of popularity around the world!

A quality breeder may breed only one or two litters a year, or they may have puppies fairly frequently. The number of puppies produced is not the issue; it is the care which is put into the breeding and into developing a breeding program. It is how knowledgeable they are about their bloodlines and how willing they are to provide you with both positive and negative information about the breed and their lines.

All puppies are wonderful. They have the same cuteness about them that babies have, but like babies, not everyone is ready to take on the responsibility of raising a puppy. Puppies take time and special attention. They will make mistakes — not just in house training but in deciding what is proper to chew and when to come and when to follow their own curiosity. They may be exuberant about life and playful when you are tired and want to settle into a chair and relax.

Evaluate your situation carefully. Frequently, people with new families will want to raise a puppy with the baby. But the caregiver for the baby may be taxed to the limit and may not be eager to take on another living being. An older dog which already has some training may be an excellent choice.

Often a breeding and show kennel may keep a dog to see how it will turn out in the show ring, only to find that it did not turn out to be the top winner they were looking for. Remember, breeders tend to sell their pet pups first, those who are most recognizable as pets, with visible show flaws. Better quality pups are kept until the breeder can get a good idea of what they will become. All show breeders are looking for that once-in-a-lifetime Best in Show dog! Buyers often call a breeder and find out they have an older puppy or young adult. The question most often asked is "What is wrong with this puppy? Why do you still have him? Why couldn't you sell him?" The answer is usually simple. For some reason the breeder thought this pup had tremendous potential. He may be a repeat of a very successful breeding. He may have been the pick of the litter. He may be the image of a top winning sire or dam as a puppy. But

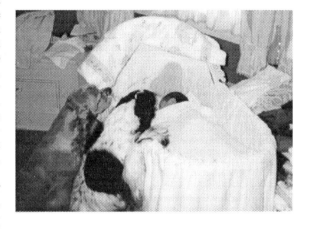

he may not turn out to be quite as good as expected — which still may make him better than ninety percent of his breed. So he is available to a good home. Breeding show dogs is an exercise in pursuing perfection. Close is often not good enough for the breeder, but it is an excellent buy for the upscale pet owner who wants a wonderful, beautiful example of the breed.

These older pups or young adults are well socialized, used to people and new situations, fine quality, and well mannered. They are leash trained, and usually crate trained. They are usually good travelers, especially if they have shown some. This may be a wonderful alternative to a puppy for homes with working adults, new babies, or people who travel a good deal.

Another decision to make is whether you are looking for a male or a female. Our breeders did not think that one sex made a better pet than another. It depends on the home situation and the family. Males may be more stable in temperament because they do not have the heat cycles and temperament changes attributable to that cycle. If a bitch is spayed, those cycles will be eliminated. Popular demand for one sex over the other may make one sex more expensive than the other. *Most of our breeders advocated neutering and spaying as part of responsible pet ownership.* Contrary to folklore, spaying and neutering will not change the temperament, nor cause an animal to get fat. It *will* reduce the chances of some types of cancer, and ensure that an unwanted litter will not be born.

Color is another matter of decision. Although you may decide that you want a particular color, it should never be the deciding factor. Find a good dog which will fit your family and your lifestyle and accept the color of the dog as a secondary factor in your decision.

Decide ahead of time who in the family is responsible for the dog in terms of training, care and exercise. The monetary cost in dog food, veterinary care and other maintenance such as shampoo and conditioners, crates and toys will be around $500 a year, though sometimes veterinary costs may run quite a bit higher if you do not take the time to get a healthy dog.

You should decide what you will do about training your dog. How will you handle housetraining? How much time can you put into it? Cockers are one of the more difficult breeds to housetrain since they tend to get involved in other things and forget they need to go out until it is too late. Training and socializing are also important and a good training class is highly recommended by most of our breeders. A well mannered dog is much more pleasant to live with than one which is excitable and unruly. Buying the right dog is the first step, but the training and time you put into raising a puppy will pay off in dividends over the years to come.

THE STANDARD

E very breed which shows anywhere in the world has a written Standard of the Breed by which the dog is judged. This standard is important in preserving "breed type," or in layman's terms, those characteristics which make an American Cocker Spaniel an American Cocker Spaniel and not a Labrador Retriever!

The Standard is revised from time to time, and may vary from one country to another, but the main portion of the standard will remain remarkably similar because they are describing the same breed. Individual dogs may vary from country to country, from one area of the country to another, and even from kennel to kennel. When a Standard is revised, only small, technical changes will be made. These changes are usually important to show breeders, but not of particular importance to the general fancier of the breed, field kennels or pet owners. Even when the Standard is changed, an American Cocker Spaniel will still look like an American Cocker Spaniel.

The Standard for the American Cocker Spaniel was changed and adapted to fit the new AKC uniform format for Breed Standards. It went into effect June 30, 1992.

General Appearance

The Cocker Spaniel is the smallest member of the Sporting Group. He has a sturdy, compact body and a cleanly chiseled and refined head, with the overall dog in complete balance and of ideal size. He stands well up at the shoulder on straight forelegs with a topline sloping slightly toward strong, moderately bent, muscular quarters. He is a dog capable of considerable speed, combined with great endurance. Above all, he must be free and merry, sound, well balanced throughout and in action show a keen inclination to work. A dog well balanced in all parts is more desirable than a dog with strongly contrasting good points and faults.

Size, Proportion, Substance

Size - The ideal height at the withers for an adult dog is 15 inches and for an adult bitch, 14 inches. Height may vary one half inch above or below this ideal. A dog whose height exceeds 15 1/2 inches or a bitch whose height exceeds 14 1/2 inches shall be disqualified. An adult dog whose height is less than 14 1/2 inches and an adult bitch whose height is less than 13 1/2 inches shall be penalized. Height is determined by a line perpendicular to the ground from the top of the shoulder blades, the dog standing naturally with its forelegs and lower hind legs parallel to the line of measurement.

Proportion - The measurement from the breast bone to back of thigh is slightly longer than the measurement from the highest point of withers to the ground. The body must be of sufficient length to permit a straight and free stride; the dog never appears long and low.

Head

To attain a well proportioned head, which must be in balance with the rest of the dog, it embodies the following: **Expression** - The expression is intelligent, alert, soft and appealing. **Eyes** - Eyeballs are round and full and look directly forward. The shape of the eye rims gives a slightly almond shaped appearance; the eye is not weak or goggled. The color of the iris is dark brown and in general the darker the better. **Ears** - Lobular, long, of fine leather, well feathered, and placed no higher than a line to the lower part of the eye. **Skull** - Rounded but not exaggerated with no tendency toward flatness; the eyebrows are clearly defined with a pronounced stop. The bony structure beneath the eyes is well chiseled with no prominence in the cheeks. The muzzle is broad and deep, with square even jaws. To be in correct balance, the distance from the stop to the tip of the nose is one half the distance from the stop up over the crown to the base of the skull. **Nose** - Of sufficient size to balance the muzzle and foreface, with well developed nostrils typical of a sporting dog. It is black in color in the blacks, black and tans, and black and whites; in other colors, it may be brown, liver or black, the darker the better. The color of nose harmonizes with the color of the eye rim. **Lips** - The upper lip is full and of sufficient depth to cover the lower jaw. **Teeth** - Strong and sound, not too small and meet in a scissor bite.

Neck, Topline, Body

Neck - The neck is sufficiently long to allow the nose to reach the ground easily, muscular and free from pendulous "throatiness." It rises strongly from the shoulders and arches slightly as it tapers to join the head. **Topline** - Sloping slightly toward muscular quarters. **Body** - The chest is deep, its lowest point no higher than the elbows, its front sufficiently wide for adequate heart and lung space, yet not so wide as to interfere with the straight forward movement of the forelegs. Ribs are deep and well sprung. Back is strong and sloping evenly and slightly downward from the shoulders to the set-on of the docked tail. The docked tail is set on and carried on a line with the topline of the back, or slightly higher; never straight up like a terrier and never so low as to indicate timidity. When the dog is in motion, the tail action is merry.

Forequarters

The shoulders are well laid back forming an angle with the upper arm of approximately 90 degrees which permits the dog to move his forelegs in an easy manner with forward reach. Shoulders are clean cut and sloping without protrusion and so set that the upper points of the withers are at an angle which permits a wide spring of rib. When viewed from the side with the forelegs vertical, the elbow is directly below the highest point of the shoulder blade. **Forelegs** - are parallel, straight, strongly boned and muscular and set close to the body well under the scapulae. The pasterns are short and strong. Dewclaws on forelegs may be removed. **Feet** - compact, large, round and firm with horny pads; they turn neither in nor out.

Hindquarters

Hips are wide and quarters well rounded and muscular. When viewed from behind, the hind legs are parallel when in motion and at rest. The hind legs are strongly boned, and muscled with moderate angulation at the stifle and powerful, clearly defined thighs. The stifle is strong and there is no slippage of it in motion or when standing. The hocks are strong and well let down. Dewclaws on hind legs may be removed.

Coat

On the head, short and fine; on the body, medium length, with enough undercoating to give protection. The ears, chest, abdomen and legs are well feathered, but not so excessively as to hide the Cocker Spaniel's true lines and movement or affect his appearance and function as a moderately coated sporting dog. The texture is most important. The coat is silky, flat or slightly wavy and of a texture which permits easy care. Excessive coat or curly or cottony textured coat shall be severely penalized. Use of electric clippers on the back coat is not desirable. Trimming to enhance the dog's true lines should be done to appear as natural as possible.

Color and Markings

Black Variety - Solid color black to include black with tan points. The black should be jet; shadings of brown or liver in the coat are not desirable. A small amount of white on the chest and/or throat is allowed; white in any other location shall disqualify. **Any Solid Color Other than**

This nice show prospect is shown at six weeks of age.

Black (ASCOB) - Any solid color other than black, ranging from lightest cream to darkest red, including brown and brown with tan points. The color shall be of a uniform shade, but lighter color of the feathering is permissible. A small amount of white on the chest and/or throat is allowed; white in any other location shall disqualify. **Parti-Color Variety** - Two or more solid, well-broken colors, one of which must be white; black and white, red and white (the red may range from lightest cream to darkest red), brown and white, and roans, to include any such color combination with tan points. It is preferable that the tan markings be located in the same pattern as for the tan points in the Black and ASCOB varieties. Roans are classified as parti-colors and may be of any of the usual roaning patterns. Primary color which is ninety percent (90%) or more shall disqualify. **Tan Points** - The color of the tan may be from the lightest cream to the darkest red and is restricted to ten percent (10%) or less of the color of the specimen; tan markings in excess of that amount shall disqualify. In the case of tan points in the Black or ASCOB variety, the markings shall be located as follows: 1. A clear tan spot over each eye; 2. On the sides of the muzzle and on the cheeks; 3. On the underside of the ears; 4. On all feet and/or legs; 5. Under the tail; 6. On the chest, optional; presence or absence shall not be penalized. Tan markings which are not readily visible or which amount only to traces, shall be penalized. Tan on the muzzle which extends upward, over and joins shall also be penalized. The absence of tan markings in the Black or ASCOB variety in any of the specified locations in any otherwise tan pointed dog shall disqualify.

Gait

The Cocker Spaniel, though the smallest of the sporting dogs, possesses a typical sporting dog gait. Prerequisite to good movement is balance between the front and rear assemblies. He drives with strong, powerful rear quarters and is properly constructed in the shoulders and forelegs so that he can reach forward without constriction in a full stride to counterbalance the driving force from the rear. Above all, his gait is coordinated, smooth and effortless. The dog must cover ground with his action; excessive animation should not be mistaken for proper gait.

Temperament

Equable in temperament with no suggestion of timidity.

Disqualifications

Height - Males over 15 1/2 inches; females over 14 1/2 inches.

Color and Markings - The aforementioned colors are the only acceptable colors or combinations of colors. Any other colors or combination of colors to disqualify.

Black Variety - White marking except on chest and throat.

Any Solid Color Other Than Black Variety - White markings except on chest and throat.

Parti-Color Variety - Primary color ninety percent (90%) or more.

Tan points - (1) Tan markings in excess of ten percent (10%); (2) Absence of tan markings in Black or ASCOB Variety in any of the specified locations in an otherwise tan pointed dog. (As published in the March, 1992, issue of the *AKC Gazette* and approved by the Board of Directors of the AKC)

All of this is a very complex way of describing what an American Cocker Spaniel should look like. It is the blueprint for the reputable breeder. Some of the terms are historical, as "lobular" ears, having been passed down with the breed from the time before it was recognized as a separate breed. Some of the terms are specific for dog show judging, or are widely ac-

The same bitch as a young adult.

cepted terms in judging animals, as "correct balance," "well let down," and "throatiness." Other terms apply to specific parts of the dog which may be unfamiliar to you such as "croup," "topline" and "feathered."

When a breeder makes a breeding, he will consider the pedigree and the individual dog. He will attempt to breed dogs which are strong in one area to dogs who are strong in other areas in the attempt to get a dog which is strong in both areas. Breeding a dog with a timid temperament or poor topline to one with similar faults, which often happens in back-yard breeding (because the breeder does not know the difference), will only result in an entire litter with the same faults!

Keep in mind that there is no perfect dog. We will talk more about this in the chapter on showing. But the dog should have the basic characteristics of the breed. If it does not, you might as well have saved your time and money as any crossbred would have done just as well as a purebred which is so poor that it does not have the basic look of the breed. If you have a Cocker already, we suggest you turn to the section called the Hall of Fame. Look at the pedigrees to see if there are any common ancestors or kennel names with your

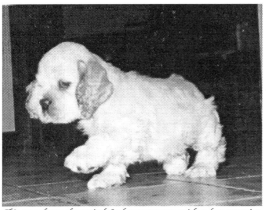

This pup shows the typical Cocker movement, with a free extension of the foreleg.

dog. Look at the photos and see how closely your dog resembles these outstanding American Cocker Spaniels. Heads are of particular importance in this breed.

In layman's terms, the standard describes a dog which is compact and well balanced; that is, no part of the dog is larger and more predominant than any other part. They are small, as described specifically in the standard, about fifteen inches for a male and fourteen inches for a female.

Our breeders tell us that the four most common reasons for a dog to be classified as a pet rather than a show dog are a soft, cottony coat, a poor head, or too much white and a bad bite. White markings can be seen almost from the time the puppy is born, and breeders will sell these dogs as pets as soon as they are old enough to leave the litter. The other faults will take longer to see. Heads, lack of substance and some other faults may be spotted by a good breeder as the dog grows to be about two to four months old. But cottony coats or bad bites may take until the dog is mature to really see. Breeders make their predictions based on what they have seen in the bloodline from previous breedings and comparison with the puppy as it grows. Even the most experienced breeder can sometimes be surprised with what a dog grows into.

Eyes of the Cocker are a focal point. They are what gives the breed its distinctive look. Those lovely Spaniel eyes are what makes you take the dog into your heart. They should be dark. Light eyes will make a dog a pet, but it will also alter his look. This is one reason why you should ask the breeder why the dog is a pet and consider if the reason will make any difference to you. Extra white may not make a difference, but light eyes will change the look and expression. On the other hand, light eyes may not be anything that bothers you, so in that case the dog will make a perfect pet for your home.

The original purpose of the American Cocker Spaniel was to hunt and retrieve in the field. He needed to pick the bird up off the ground, so his neck should be long enough to allow the nose to reach the ground, and well muscled enough to give him the strength to lift the bird and carry it back to his master. He should have enough chest and spring of ribs to be sturdy, not delicate. He should be able to move out and cover ground, so that in spite of the fact that he is small, he is fast at a trot, not slow and lumbering. These are all examples of how the original purpose of the dog contributes to the look of the breed, even when the original purpose has become secondary. Today, the American Cocker Spaniel is primarily a companion and more American Cockers show in the ring than work in the field.

The tail of the Cocker Spaniel is very important. Many of our breeders felt it was a barometer to the temperament. It should be happy, and wagging most of the time. This shows a "merry" temperament and a "willingness to work." A dog with a tail which simply hangs behind him, or one that droops, will probably have a timid temperament. One of the main problems with poorly bred Cockers is the temperament. A timid dog may become a fear biter, a trait that is most unpleasant and difficult to overcome.

One of the things you may notice about the standard is where it talks about coat. There is no mention of the coats as you will see them on the show animals featured in our Hall of Fame or on our covers. Historically, there has been no mention of that type of coat in any of the previous standards, and until recent years, American Cockers did not show in such exaggerated coats. This is an example of what has simply become fashionable in the show ring. Dogs with long, flowing coats cannot run in any field, or even in long grass, because everything becomes entangled in the long, silky hair strands. This popular show coat would certainly not be proper for the dog in the field, and it is very difficult to maintain on a daily basis. Some of our breeders who have been in the breed for many years consider this popular long show coat to be improper. Certainly it would have been considered inappropriate even for the show ring twenty years ago. Most companion dogs are kept in short, easier to care for coats. And indeed, most of our breeders reported that they cut down the coat on show dogs as soon as these dogs retired from the ring.

"Style" is a term used to describe the various individuals which still fall within the framework of the standard. Countries, geographic areas of the United States, and different kennels and bloodlines will have a different look. You can see some of these minor differences by comparing the different pictures in the Hall of Fame. Heads are the easiest to see in the photos, and a careful study will reveal differences in muzzle, for example. All of this is a way of saying that although Cocker Spaniels should look like Cocker Spaniels, not all Cocker Spaniels will look EXACTLY alike. The reason for the variety is because the standard contains many words which are open to interpretation. Words such as "slightly" "rounded but not exaggerated," "tendency toward...," and "sufficiently," give each breeder some room for judgment. Remember, we have said that no dog is perfect. One reason is because the evaluation of what is "perfect" differs from breeder to breeder and judge to judge, depending on how they interpret certain ambiguous words. Each breeder puts emphasis on different things. One breeder may be able to accept a dog with a poorer shoulder than he would like if the head and coat are good, while another may feel that movement is most

important, and will accept a head which is not so spectacular if the shoulders and movement are good.

And styles change over the years. Coats are one example of style which has changed in the last twenty years. Although the length and presentation of the coat has changed, it is the STANDARD which maintains that the TEXTURE of the coat should be silky and smooth, not soft and cottony. So the standard has been preserved, although the style which is currently popular has somewhat changed the appearance of the dog.

Breeders often start training show pups at a very early age.

FINDING A BREEDER

*I*f you have time, go to a local dog show and see all the different breeds in the ring. This can be done by going early and staying all day, wandering from ring to ring and looking at the breeds you are interested in seeing, or by going sometime in the early afternoon. Groups are held at the end of the judging day, usually starting around two o'clock, depending on the size of the show. Here, the single best representative of each breed compete in one of seven different groups. The group winners will return at the end of the day for the judging of Best in Show.

Don't expect to see puppies at a dog show. Good breeders — and AKC rules — keep puppies at home where they belong. Breeders are there for the sport, not for the purpose of selling puppies, so the attitude of breeders selling you a puppy will not be the same as those of a pet shop. In a pet shop, you are the customer because it is their business to sell you a puppy. With a breeder, this is his sport or hobby. He has no trouble selling the puppies he offers for sale each year, and he is primarily concerned with matching the puppy with the new home to ensure a long and happy relationship for both the new owner and the dog, not in getting your money. Because of that, he is less likely to act as if you are the valued customer, so remember that when you deal with a breeder. Breeders look at their pups as part of their family, and part of your family. Their role is closer to that of a social worker handling an adoption than a retail business which is selling a product to a customer. There are not two dogs alike, and they are not something which can be ordered or fixed like an inanimate object offered in a store or catalogue.

It is sometimes difficult to talk to breeders at a show because they may be busy getting their dogs ready for the ring. Most show people take these shows very seriously and therefore they may be short of small talk at the show. Remember that these exhibitors have a lot invested in the show at hand in terms of entry fees, travel and perhaps handling expenses and advertising. Selling you a puppy or helping you find one is not likely to be their first priority the day of the show.

However, a dog show is a good place to find names and addresses of breeders. A catalog of the show will list the name of the entry, the owner or owners and an address, the name of the breeder, the sire and dam of the entry, the whelping date of the entry and sometimes the name of the "agent," or person actually showing the entry on that day. By watching the classes, you can see what to expect of a Cocker Spaniel at different ages, how they develop, and by looking at sires and dams, and then looking at the dogs in the ring, you will begin to see  family resemblances in different bloodlines, much as you can see them by looking at the pictures in the Hall of Fame. You will also get to see the difference between the American

Cocker Spaniels and the English Cocker Spaniels. The address of the owner may be listed under the name of the dog, or it may be in the back of the book where all owners for all breeds of dog may be listed alphabetically. When you get home, call directory information for the phone number or write for information and a contact phone number.

Local kennel clubs may have a listing of breeders in your area. Calling breeders from some of the major dog publications is another way of beginning the process of finding a dog. We have featured breeders in the Hall of Fame who are knowledgeable in the breed and who will be willing to talk to you.

It is more important to find a breeder with whom you are comfortable than to find one close to your home. Going to visit the litter may be fun, but it may also lead to disaster. A good breeder, one who knows the bloodline and has watched the puppies from birth, will have a better idea of what will fit your lifestyle. Describe HOW you want the dog to fit into your household, what you expect it to do, and what your family is like. Ask the breeder how he or she feels on issues of importance to you. Listen carefully to the answers. Ask the breeder to list the most important factors in their breeding program. If health (or soundness) and temperament are not on the list — be careful. Then listen for those qualities you think will be important to you, such as intelligence, show quality, size and potential for training.

Each breeder will have his own ideas about what is the most important thing in a Cocker, or in other words the "essence" of the breed. One breeder will focus on good coats, while another will focus on good heads. Each will select their breeding stock based on the area of importance to them. When a breeder adds new stock to his program, makes an "outside" breeding (one to a stud or bitch which is not owned by the kennel), or selects puppies to keep for the breeding and show program, the breeder will select animals which are strong in those areas of importance. That is why you will see a difference between kennels. This difference is referred to as "style."

Read through the Hall of Fame information. See if what the breeder says about his breeding program matches what you are looking for in a dog. When you talk to him on the phone, ask about his philosophy of breeding. Many breeders will simply say, "We breed for . . ." See if he or she is breeding for what you need in a dog.

In the end, you are often better off trusting the breeder to select a puppy for your family than in picking it yourself. You will see the puppies for only a short time. One may be tired after a morning of playing, it may have just eaten and be sleepy, or it may be awakened or be reacting to a littermate in an uncharacteristic manner. Puppies are like all siblings; they do not always bring out the best in one another, though generally they will get along.

The breeder has seen this litter for weeks, watching it and comparing it to other litters from the same bloodlines. He knows more about each puppy from past experience than you can possibly see within the framework of a short visit. Remember, the selection you make will be with you for many years and it should be based on sound judgment and as much information as you can find out before making the selection. This is a little like going to a stock broker, lawyer or insurance agent for advice rather than trying to handle such matters yourself by a quick, often ignorant evaluation of what is going on.

WHAT TO ASK A BREEDER

Be sure to identify the qualities you want in a dog. Because temperament varies within the breed, between kennels, and between individuals, ask about how the breeder views the temperament of the breed in general, and this litter in particular. See how well the answers match your family's needs.

Don't seek conflicting qualities. An active, playful, outgoing dog is apt to be harder to train and harder on the house than one with a laid back personality which is basically quiet by nature. Cockers, in general, are active and merry. They will need firm, kind discipline from the beginning. If you have a house full of antiques, it is best not to look for the puppy who is the clown of the litter. He will be the one who will likely steal socks, carry off the toilet paper (which is still attached to the roll in the bathroom), rearrange the dried flower arrangement, and reconstruct the antique chair legs. Select the more sedate littermate who is more interested in being a quiet, human companion. If you have young children, don't select the feisty one. If he stands up for his rights with his littermates, he may also stand up for his rights to the food bowl and toys if the baby approaches.

Cockers are busy and curious. They will open doors and look in, and if left undisciplined, they may inspect the top of the kitchen table to see what has been left there. They may be avid gardeners, rearranging the flower beds enthusiastically. Ask your breeder and prepare yourself to do early training with the puppy or new dog so that you can get off to a good, sound start in the relationship.

Cockers adapt to a variety of homes as long as they have human companionship. They do not need a large yard, but they do need exercise on a regular basis. They are small enough to be suitable for apartments, but must be taken for frequent walks. They may prefer one member of the family over another, but will often switch their affections if a different family member takes over the feeding and exercise. They love to be petted and played with, using almost any sort of play activity or toy.

Ask the breeder what health problems may be present in the breed. If the breeder continuously states that there are no problems in health or temperament, no problems in training, and generally represents the dog to be nothing but a 100% ideal pet, beautiful enough to be a show dog but "I just want to find him a good home," be careful. While all responsible breeders are interested in finding their puppies a good home, they should also be able to evaluate their dogs and alert you to what you need to be aware of in dog ownership and ownership of a Cocker Spaniel in particular. Individual dogs need training and socialization. Bloodlines have good points and bad points, and a good breeder will know both the strengths and weaknesses. "Kennel blind" breeders may run the risk of overlooking faults and thereby breeding them into the line. A breeder cannot strive to eliminate a problem if he is too kennel blind to see it.

If you are looking for a pet, be sure to ask WHY the puppy is selling as a pet. Be careful of breeders who give involved stories about why this is a perfect dog, but is being sold at a bargain price. As in any other field, these people know their product. Most reasons for a dog to be classified as a pet are of no concern to the average pet owner. A good breeder is producing dogs of such high quality that the small, critical points which will cause him to sell the dog as a pet will hardly be recognized at all by the average owner. The poorest quality dog from a good breeder will still be miles above those produced by a backyard breeder or a puppy mill.

Think of it in terms of basketball. If you are watching junior high school basketball, you may be able to pick out the best player. But that player will be infinitely inferior to an NBA player who has been dropped off the team for his lack of ability! Such is the difference between a puppy which is being cut by a breeder and sold as a pet (the professional player who has been dropped) and the best of what the backyard breeder or puppy mill will produce. Pets from a good breeder will run $400 to $500, with show dogs going higher, depending on their age and quality. You will pay the same from a pet shop. You may buy a pup from a backyard breeder for only $150 but consider that American Cocker Spaniels live for twelve to fifteen years. One of our breeders reported a top producing male who was still active, producing puppies, and in perfect health at eleven and a half years. If you divide the extra cost by the number of years of the dog, you are paying $16 to $20 more per year to have a really beautiful dog in good health and with a good temperament! It is like owning a Mercedes instead of a Geo Metro for only about $20 a year!

And, you may not even save that on a lower priced dog. Health problems, which the backyard breeder may be ignorant of, or the puppy mill breeder may not care about, may run the vet bills up much higher over the lifetime of the dog than the additional price of the dog.

When considering sex, realize that a bitch will have, as one breeder said, "raging hormones." This may cause her to have mood swings and to lose coat. If spayed, which most of our breeders highly recommended, this problem will be eliminated. If you are looking to keep down the cost of a dog, consider that neutering a male is cheaper than spaying a female.

Older dogs may be an alternative. Cockers adapt to almost any type of home, and an older, well mannered, well socialized dog may be an alternative if the family does not have a lot of time or patience for a puppy. If household members are not home during the day, if you are looking for a dog which is ready to play, travel, or show, you should look for an older dog. Pups need care, training, rest, and should not be taken out in public until after they have had a full set of shots. They may be too delicate or tire easily when playing with older children. If you are looking for a show dog, try to find an older dog which can be evaluated in terms of the finer points of conformation and movement. The older the dog is, and the more successful his parents and other litters of the same breeding have been, the higher the chances that he will be a show ring winner. Sometimes a breeder will keep two littermate brothers until they are old enough to see some fine

points of adult conformation. Then the lesser brother will be sold to make room in the kennel. These dogs are a good buy because they are the very best of the litter.

Common show faults which will make a dog a pet are: off-bites (which may not show up until the permanent teeth are in), slip stifles (ask about this carefully and see the "health" chapter), low tail set, weak topline or high ear set (which will go almost undetected to anyone but a show breeder or judge), mismarking or undesirable show color, light eyes (as we have mentioned in the chapter on the standard), length of back, low in the leg, high in the rear, lack of substance or having restricted movement. Breeders will also talk about such things as "terrier fronts" which are becoming a problem for show breeders, poor shoulder angulation, and lack of extension when moving. Unless you have spent years with show dogs, these faults will be hard to see even if they are pointed out to you, though to the breeder they may be very obvious.

Likewise, if you want a good looking, top quality dog, even if it is for a pet, do not expect a small price tag simply because you don't want to show. Often the same qualities which make an attractive dog a good show prospect also make it a particularly appealing pet. Remember, breeders price their puppies by quality or characteristics, not for purposes of the buyer. However, some breeders may insist that certain puppies be shown as part of the buying contract. Be sure to inquire about show contracts if you are seeking a top quality dog which is represented as being a show prospect. Also, sales of bitch puppies sometimes include a demand for puppies back to the breeder as part of the purchase price. Think about this carefully. It will obligate you to working with the breeder for many years to come, and commits you to breeding a litter of puppies in the future when you may not want to do so.

You get all the work of raising a litter, (see last chapter on "Breeding Your Dog") and the breeder gets the best puppy or puppies!

If you are interested in showing or breeding the dog, you need to be honest about that up front. Don't try to get a show dog for a cheap price because you say it will be a pet. The worst possible thing to do is to tell a breeder you only want a pet, when in fact you have intentions of breeding it. First, consider carefully before you breed you dog. As we have outlined in the last chapter, it may not be the quick and easy money it looks like, nor the wonderful experience you envision. Second, there may be problems with the dog which the breeder did not reveal because it would not affect your puppy, but which would make it inadvisable to breed the dog. Littermates may have carried defects which were problems. Although your dog may not be affected by the problem and it was not mentioned by the breeder since your dog was healthy, the breeder may sell the litter as pets because he realizes that there is a high chance the normal pups may carry the recessive gene and pass it along to their offspring. Then YOU are the breeder who has to deal with the problem which may be costly, result in loss of puppies or irate buyers who may purchase pups with problems that you do not have the experience to spot!

So, if you intend to breed, or even think you may breed, tell the breeder up front. Invest the money in a good dog or bitch. Be honest about what you want to do with the dog as this is the only way a breeder can do his job in helping you find the right dog for you and your family. Today AKC will allow breeders to mark papers as "non-breeding," which means that even though the dog or bitch you have purchased may carry AKC papers, puppies from that animal may not be registered, even if bred to another AKC registered animal. You, as the new owner, cannot change the registration after the purchase. This has been done to try to eliminate backyard breeding and every year more breeders use this option for their pet puppies. (See chapter on "Paperwork" for more information on this limited registration.)

Ask the breeder about spaying and neutering contracts. Ask what guarantee the breeder offers with the puppy. CAUTION: If you are seeking a show dog, don't expect a breeder to be able to pick out a group placing dog at eight weeks of age. These are few and far between, and a show dog is a product not only of his gene pool, but of environmental factors in his upbringing, how he is shown and conditioned, how he is presented in the ring, where he is shown, and what other dogs he is showing against on any given day.

Remember, if you are looking for a field or show ring winner, find a pedigree where the parents, other litters, and other dogs in the litter have excelled in the field or ring. That is your best assurance that the puppy is likely to be successful in competition. Better yet, find an older puppy or young adult that can be evaluated in the ring or in the field.

Look at other adults in the kennel if you visit. See if they look like the kind of dog you are looking for. See the dam, and if possible, see the sire of the litter. These are usually a good indication of quality and characteristics of the puppy. One word of caution: After a bitch whelps, she may lose her hair. This is called "blowing coat." Some bitches do it worse than others so that you may hardly notice it on one bitch, yet another may look ratty and have bald spots. This is NOT an indication of skin problems. It does not mean that the pups will have skin problems. It is a psysiological condition which is sometimes apparent in bitches after whelping. It is brought on by hormones released during whelping and lactation. Many breeders believe that it is caused by the protein which would normally go to hair growth being redirected to the milk for the puppies. If you see a bitch whose coat is in "ratty" condition, ask your breeder about it, but realize that it may be normal for this bitch.

BUYING A DOG LONG DISTANCE

Sometimes it is necessary to buy a dog a long distance. Don't panic. When you talk to a breeder on the phone, use the same technique you would use in person. Ask questions that will give you an idea of the experience of your breeder; how they feel about issues in the breed that are important to you and your family; how well they listen to why you want the dog; and how well they try to match you with what they have available. Find one who enjoys his dogs, who knows what his bloodlines will produce, and who sounds like someone you can trust and have confidence in. Ask about guarantees and expectations. This is the same thing you should be doing with a local breeder, or one whose kennel you visit to see a litter.

WHAT NOT TO ASK A BREEDER

Don't ask a breeder what he thinks of another breeder by name. Ask for a reference if he has nothing available, but when you ask about another breeder by name, you may get

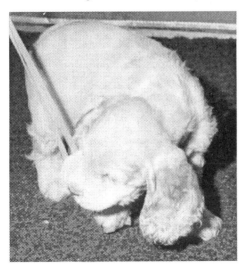

more information about the politics within the breed and personal prejudices, both for and against, than real information about the quality of dogs being bred. One breeder may like a small dog and have nothing good to say about another breeder's larger dogs, without really giving the reason why there is a negative comment. Remember that dog breeding, showing and field trial competitions are just that — competitions. Over the years, disputes arise over wins and losses, or over personal stories that may have nothing to do with the quality of the dog or the purpose you have in mind for your pet. These "feuds" are carried over into what one breeder — and later his close friends — say about another breeder.

Do not expect to be able to go to a breeder's home for a Sunday visit if you are simply looking at the breed for future reference. While some breeders have this kind of time, most show and field trial breeders do not have hours to spend on people who visit as something to do for the day. If you are simply looking at the breed, you can do that at a dog show where you can see many examples of the breed.

Do not expect to handle a litter of puppies, even if you are ready to buy. Many diseases are transmittable through handling and the breeder has no way of knowing what you have been exposed to and may be carrying in terms of dog diseases. A breeder may ask you to only look at the puppies, not to touch them. Breeders do not have the kind of inflated prices, nor the callousness, which allows them to simply write off the death of a puppy from over-handling, or being exposed to something a visitor may be unknowingly carrying.

Do not expect to view a litter shortly after birth. Most breeders will limit viewing to puppies which have been weaned and are ready to go home. While it is a good idea to see the dam and the sire if possible, so that you have a good idea of what the puppy may grow

up to look like, strangers around very young litters (under five weeks) may irritate the bitch, and unless you are very familiar with the bloodline, you will probably not be able to see anything more than a cute lump!

Finally, often breeders will begin to sell their pups at or shortly before birth. So don't expect to go and have the pick of the litter. A breeder who is really doing his job listens carefully to what each buyer is looking for and matches the puppy to the home. If the litter has, for example, five pups, one or all of them may be sold before they are eight weeks old. You may go to the kennel and fall in love with a puppy only to find it has been sold to someone who put their faith in the breeder at or around the time the litter was born. Different breeders handle this differently, but don't be surprised to find that if you want to see the litter before you buy, all or most of the pups may be sold before you get a chance to see them.

WHAT A BREEDER MAY ASK YOU

Besides questions about your household, most breeders will want to know if you have any plans for training, exercise and socialization. They will make recommendations based on what they believe are the needs of their dogs. They may ask if you intend to spay or neuter the puppy and at what age. They will ask you about other animals in your home, and what experience you have had with dogs in the past. They will want to know if your yard is fenced, what kind of living pattern you have and who comes in and out of the house on a regular basis. They may want to know what your work schedule is and even if you are planning a family. Don't look at these questions as an invasion of privacy. The breeder is trying to determine if the breed, the bloodline and the puppy are right for you and your home. Almost every reputable breeder we talked to said that there had been people they simply refused to sell to because they did not think the dog, or in some cases even the breed, was the right fit. Through their years of labor and experience, breeders are trying to save you time, money and emotional problems by getting the right dog into the right home.

A breeder may ask that you have the puppy checked by your local veterinarian so that everyone can feel confident about the health of the puppy. (Do not expect most veterinarians to be experts on the finer points of conformation.)

WHAT A BREEDER SHOULD OFFER

Look for a breeder who is enthusiastic in talking about his dogs. A good breeder has put a lot of time and money into his breeding program. It is natural that he or she will talk freely and with knowledge about the pedigree, the individuals they own, and about the breed in general.

A breeder should offer a kennel pedigree of the dog. AKC will provide a certified copy of the actual pedigree for a fee, but breeders will usually give at least a handwritten copy with the puppy. This is not a certified pedigree, but it should be accurate based on the breeder's kennel records. Champions should be marked, and sometimes other information such as color or CERF (see chapter on Health) certification is provided.

A breeder should offer some kind of proof that the breeding stock is free of hereditary diseases, and/or some guarantee if the puppy does not turn out to be free of such problems. However, don't expect more than you buy. A breeder may offer a guarantee for

genetic defects which will affect the use of the dog, as it is purchased. If a dog is purchased as a show and/or breeding dog, and only one testicle descends for example, this would make the dog ineligible to show, and basically unbreedable. A guarantee of replacement or some kind of refund, depending on the breeder, should certainly apply since the dog could not fulfill the original purpose for which he was purchased. (Dogs with one testicle can reproduce, but it is a fault which will be passed on to the offspring and therefore the dog SHOULD not be bred.) If the dog was sold as a pet, there would be no guarantee for the problem since it does not affect in any way the dog's general health or ability to be a companion. Most breeders advise neutering pets, and therefore the single testicle would make no difference.

A breeder should give you a record of the shots and worming that the puppy has had. Puppies should not leave a breeder without at least one set of shots, and most breeders automatically worm puppies. Puppies, like babies, put everything in their mouths so it is very easy for them to pick up parasites.

A breeder should offer instructions on what to feed the pup and how to care for it. Remember that no breeder is infallible. Even with the best of care and knowledge, a puppy may have a health or temperament problem. Breeders will usually not refund money, but many breeders will work with you to replace or exchange a puppy with a problem. Guarantees are usually less broad on an adult dog because health, temperament and conformation problems are easy to identify.

One legitimate reason many breeders do not give money back is because this makes the dog more of an investment for the new owner than a member of the family. If breeders were to offer money back, they would be functioning as a savings bank, allowing the dog to be returned for the purchase price any time the new owner felt they no longer wanted the dog, or any time they needed money. There is often a *lot* of difference in opinion about *how much* a partial refund should be and *how bad* the problem really is and *what part* of the blame is rightfully that of the breeder and what part is rightfully the blame of the owner. For all of these reasons, breeders usually prefer their dogs to go into homes where they will be appreciated and loved as members of the family. If the purpose of the buyer is truly to own a nice dog, then a replacement is the logical solution, still giving the owner what he wanted in the first place — a loving, healthy pet.

A breeder will ask you to call and let him know how the puppy is doing, how it is getting along in the new home, and what it grows up to be. Remember, sending photos of the dog in his new home, and again when he is an adult is a very nice way of saying "thank you" to your breeder. Like proud parents, most breeders want to know what happens to their pups, and what kind of adults they turn out to be. It is also a way for them to check how well their breeding program is working. Most of our breeders said they wished people would remember to do this. A photo at Christmas, on the dog's birthday, or any time you have an extra one, is a wonderful present to any breeder truly interested in his dogs.

HEALTH

*H*eredity problems are a fact of life in almost all dog breeds. Again, the reason to buy a pedigree dog from a good breeder is that you have some idea of what kinds of health problems you may face, and how likely they are to show up in individuals.

Eyes - By far the most common health problem reported by our breeders was Progressive Retinal Atrophy (PRA). This is a complex disease consisting of several inherited photoreceptor diseases that have a similar clinical appearance. It is a recessive trait in various dog breeds, including the Cocker Spaniel. The age of onset of clinical signs varies with the type of PRA. It can show up as early as four to six months, or as late as six or seven years. For this reason, an annual check is necessary. Dogs must be tested every year because it is possible for a dog to be clear of PRA in youth, only to develop the disease later in life. Most of our breeders did an annual check of their breeding stock, and knew the incidence of it in their bloodlines. Animals with evidence of eye disease should not be bred.

Night blindness is noted early and progresses to total blindness over a period of months to years. Progressive cortical cataracts are common later in the course of PRA and may mask the underlying retinopathy. No effective therapy is available.

There are a number of clinics and ophthalmologists who can perform an examination to uncover these problems. A certificate, called a CERF certificate, can be issued for the dog by sending clear findings to the Canine Eye Registration Foundation for issuance of a CERF number. Be sure to ask you breeder if their stock has been examined, and how long ago the examination took place.

Hips and Patellas - Although the most common term heard concerning dog's health is hip dysplasia, the Cocker Spaniel is a small breed, with a compact build, and it is typical that smaller, well proportioned dogs are not troubled by hip problems. None of our breeders mentioned hips. It may be possible that some Cockers are radiographically dysplastic, without being physically dysplastic. That is to say, that if the hips are X-rayed, they may not fit the strict criteria for bone structure, but due to the size and body build of the Cocker Spaniel, there are seldom if ever physical problems connected with the joint configuration. In such cases, breeders usually do not concern themselves with the problem.

More common are patella problems. The patella is the rear joint similar to the knee cap in humans. It may move out of place and cause pain — a condition called a "luxating patella." In severe cases it may require an operation to stabilize it. Such operations are expensive, often running $300 to $500. Be sure to ask your breeder about the incidence of patella problems in his or her bloodline.

Skin Problems - One of the most frustrating health problems can be skin infections and conditions. Several of our breeders reported that skin problems in Cockers are found frequently in certain bloodlines. Causes and severity of the condition vary greatly between dogs. This is something you should be sure to ask your breeder about.

Most diseases are carried as recessive genes. It is possible that both parents can be free of the disease, but be carriers. Buyers should always ask the breeder about the soundness of the complete bloodline. Be sure to ask what, if any, guarantee is being offered.

Inbreeding and line breeding are often confused with health problems. This is not true in itself. They can also be your assurance that you will NOT have a particular problem.

An inbred dog, one with several close breedings such as sister to brother, father to daughter, dam to son, etc. will be likely to produce more puppies with recessive traits. Recessive traits need to be carried on both sides in order to exhibit themselves in the puppy. If you are breeding the same recessive traits over and over again, the more likely they are to surface. The same is true, though to a lesser extent, in line breeding, where lines are bred back and forth using similarly bred animals who may not be direct relatives in the first generation or two. The difference between line breeding and inbreeding is the NUMBER of animals used in the gene pool, and how closely they are bred.

If a line is free of health problems, line breeding and inbreeding ensure that the puppies will be clear because there is no way for the recessive, offending gene to enter the gene pool. This is the argument breeders have against outcrossing. Introducing a new blood-line which may carry the unwanted recessive gene may be considered too much of a risk to them. But if the gene pool carries the offending gene, line breeding and certainly inbreeding will increase the chances of it turning up. Because recessive genes are impossible to identify by looking at the dog, breeders often do test breedings of close relatives to see if the trait will show up. It is their way of "testing" their gene pool.

Although line breeding and inbreeding are part of the intricate study of genetics, and something breeders spend their lives learning about, it is sufficient to realize that the practice of line breeding and inbreeding is no better and no worse than the quality of the stock from which the breeder started breeding. In itself, the practice does not mean that the puppies will be healthy or unhealthy, crazy or calm, large or small. It simply means that whatever recessive genes are lurking under the surface, the tighter the breeding, the more likely they are to manifest themselves in the puppies.

PUPPY SHOTS AND PUPPY HEALTH CARE

Your puppy will come to you with vaccinations. But be prepared that these days, with rapidly mutating virus strains, the pattern of vaccinations may be different than it was a number of years ago. And you may find more variety of opinion than you did if your last puppy was fifteen or twenty years ago.

Some breeders begin to vaccinate very early. Others wait until a few weeks later. Some believe in the new "Fort Dodge KF-11 shots." Others think this shot is nothing more than pharmaceutical company hype. Norden has a "First Dose" which is suppose to take effect AROUND the mother's immunity, and it eliminates the middle puppy shot. Get a copy of the kind of shots, and the dates the puppy has received them, and take them to the vet. If your vet comments about the shots, remember that vaccination schedules are becoming more controversial every year. Our advice is to find a vet you feel comfortable with, and fall into line with whatever he suggests. The fact is that puppies survive and prosper under a number of different programs; the important thing is to be sure that vaccinations are given.

Traditionally, puppies were given a six-way vaccination at eight weeks, twelve weeks and sixteen weeks. This is not because it takes three vaccinations to develop an immunity, but because puppies are born with an immunity from their mother. This maternal immunity wears off some time between eight weeks and four months. If the vaccination is given too early, the immunity of the mother goes into effect, throws off the vaccine, and blocks the development of independent immunity in the puppy. Therefore, if a vaccination is given every month until four months of age, the odds are that sometime in that period, the mother's immunity will wear off, and the puppy will develop his own, independent immunity as a result of the vaccine. Further vaccinations are simply thrown off because the puppy has immunity of his own, much as the maternal immunity blocked the immunity of the puppy at an earlier age. The final vaccination is always given AFTER four months, as that is the longest possible time that maternal immunity will last. At that point, the puppy will be ready to develop his own immunity. However, if the puppy is given a vaccination at

eight weeks, and still has maternal immunity, and that maternal immunity wears off at say, ten or twelve weeks, he is left with no immunity. If shots were not given again until sixteen weeks, that would leave the puppy without immunity between the time the mother's immunity wore off at ten weeks, and the new shot was given at sixteen weeks.

Puppy shots are generally given for distemper, hepatitileptospirosis and parainfluenza, Adenovirus Type 2 and parvo. Some breeders also give bordatella and/or corona vaccines, and some no longer give leptospirosis. Today, vets can buy shots in almost any combination. No matter what the combination you, your breeder and your vet decide upon, you will need to repeat it once a year for the rest of the dog's life in order to ensure that he will maintain the immunity he needs.

Rabies vaccinations work much the same way, except that only the mature shot is given. Some states and vets require that shots be given at four months of age. Others are of the opinion that four months is too young, and they prefer to give the rabies vaccination after six months of age. Although DHLP and other vaccinations may be given by breeders, almost every state requires that rabies vaccinations be given and documented by a veterinarian. Lyme disease and heartworm treatment will vary from one region of the country to another and from veterinarian to veterinarian. We suggest you discuss appropriate vaccinations and preventatives with your family veterinarian, who knows what is necessary for your area.

Most of our breeders recommended that you do not expose the puppy to any other un-inoculated dogs until after the final puppy shot at four months of age. This means that he should not visit friends and relatives with dogs, he should not go to public parks and walkways, or any other area with heavy dog traffic. Even after inoculation, the titer (immunity in the blood) does not reach safe levels for approximately ten days after the vaccinations.

Puppies are like babies; they pick up everything they see and put it in their mouths. This is their way of acquainting themselves with their universe. Cockers are curious by nature, and originally a retrieving breed. This means that they are even more prone to pick up things in their mouths and carry them around. The result is that they are very likely to infest themselves with parasites. A puppy may come to you worm-free, or he may have some worms even with a careful worming program on the part of the breeder. If your puppy comes from a warm, humid climate, the chances are higher that he will have worms when he arrives. In some parts of the country, even careful breeders with aggressive worming programs may have a problem. In dry climates with cold winters such as the Rocky Mountains there is far less of a parasite problem. In any case, he will most certainly pick up worms during his puppyhood simply from things in the environment which he will "taste", and which are contaminated. Some vets prefer to simply worm puppies on a regular basis, and others prefer to test stool samples to establish what type of parasites exist and the extent is of infestation. Climates, living conditions, and soil conditions make a difference in the frequency of all types of parasites.

SELECTING A VET

One of the most important things you will do is to select a vet. Like doctors, not all vets are alike in their attitudes and treatment programs. Don't be alarmed if your breeder does not accept everything your vet may say about the puppy as the absolute truth. Veteri-

nary medicine, just like human medicine, is not an exact science; accept that. Breeders have been working with the same genetic pool for many years; the vet comes into the room and sees the puppy for the first time, often without a strong background in either the breed or the bloodline, and he may be unaware of peculiarities common to the breed or bloodline and may interpret them as a health problem.

Although most vets are careful professionals, breeders have some recommendations in selecting a vet. If your vet, either with a previous dog, or with your new dog, begins to suggest rare conditions and complicated health problems, they suggest you get a second opinion. This is simply good practice, especially if treatments are costly. Call your breeder and ask if the condition is something to reasonably expect from the bloodline. And don't get the second opinion from another vet in the same office. People who work together often take the same approach to a problem. This makes for good working conditions, but it does not give a true second opinion.

Second, if your vet begins to make wide sweeping generalizations about the breed and your dog — especially on the first visit — think twice about what he is saying. Seldom are vets experts in any specific breed. Even if they happen to be breeders themselves, they may have only a working knowledge of other breeds based on the dogs of that breed that they see in their practice. Vets often see a vastly greater number of dogs with health problems than well dogs. Well dogs only visit the vet once a year for shots, while sickly dogs may be frequent visitors. We forget that by virtue of what they do, vets see a disproportionate number of sick and unhealthy dogs! Vets sometimes base their opinion of a breed on the few dogs they see on a regular basis which have excessive health problems. Or, there may be a backyard breeder in the area producing dogs with health problems which are not typical of well-bred examples of the breed.

As an owner, it is your job to see that your Cocker is well trained and well behaved at all times, including those times he visits the vet. Be sure that he is under control and has a good attitude toward strangers, even the vet. This can be accomplished by steady discipline and good socialization from the time the dog enters your home.

HOLISTIC MEDICINE AS AN ALTERNATIVE

Recently, people have become very interested in natural healing alternatives commonly referred to as "holistic," "complementary" or "alternative" medicines. Acupuncture, chiropractic, nutrition, herbs and homeopathy are the most widespread alternative therapies available. This interest is expanding rapidly into the world of pets. Conventional medicine follows a reductionist philosophy, focusing on what is considered the exact location or cause of disease and attempting to remove it, kill it or suppress it. For example, antibiotics are used to kill germs, tumors are removed or destroyed and allergic reactions are suppressed with drugs.

Practitioners of holistic or alternative medicines feel the problem is that none of these therapies address the real reasons the pet is sick. Healthy animals do not get serious infections, tumors or allergies. A pet's immune system is malfunctioning BEFORE these "diseases" occur. Therefore, what needs to be addressed is the functioning of the ENTIRE body, mind and spirit of the pet. Through this approach, the whole body functions better and it can prevent or cure almost anything, according to those who practice holistic medicine.

Vaccination has become a focus for some practitioners of holistic medicine. Noting that some puppies develop the diseases for which they have recently been inoculated, some believe that elimination of such vaccinations is an alternative. Other breeders prefer to space out their vaccinations, or not to give them in combinations. Some believe that annual boosters are NOT necessary, especially for dogs with other medical problems. The serious followers of holistic medicines feel that good nutrition and homeopathy can prevent these conditions as well if not better than vaccination. **IT IS IMPORTANT TO NOTE THAT SIMPLY FORGOING VACCINATIONS IS NOT THE ANSWER.** *If you are interested in holistic medicine, take the time, learn more about it, and tailor it to your dog, his needs, and your ability to provide the necessary program.* Holistic medicine as a prevention of disease is based on maintaining good health through a number of different applications, ALL of which must be carefully maintained in order for the program to work! There are a number of breeders and owners who believe the health of their pets have been improved with such practices.

Nutrition - There is a wide variety of opinions on dog nutrition which has often led to conflicting nutritional programs. Food preservatives have been blamed by some for some allergic reactions. Others feel that pets suffer as a direct result of inadequate and even toxic pet foods. Still others feel that food must be fed as it is in nature — RAW and including organs and glands, bones, vegetables, live digestive bacteria and active enzymes. Almost all of these schools of thought believe that natural nutrition can improve virtually any condition and by itself cure a great many. Additives, such as the Blue Green Algae mentioned in our Shopping Arcade section, have been found by some breeders to improve the quality of life from improving temperament and energy levels to eliminating skin or immune problems.

Acupuncture - Acupuncture has been used for thousands of years. The life energy of the body (chi) flows through a series of channels (meridians). This energy is responsible for maintaining health and body functions. The energy may become excessive, deficient or blocked. There are points along the meridians through which the energy flow can be adjusted. This is usually accomplished through the use of needles. Lasers and pressure (acupressure) may also be used. Balancing and restoring energy flow can result in tremendous health benefits. With the improved health, diseases are eliminated.

Chiropractic - The central nervous system is a major communications system within the body. Interference with nerve function can result in a tremendous number of symptoms. Physical and emotional stresses cause misalignment of spinal bones and impeded nerve communication. Chiropractic adjustments restore proper nervous system function, resulting in the elimination of a variety of health problems. There is another benefit to chiropractic that is not often discussed. Three acupuncture meridians (see above) run along and beside the spinal bones. Therefore, realigning the spine allows better energy flow.

Herb - There are different systems of herbal medicine in use: Chinese, Western and Ayurvedic (from India). The Chinese and Ayurvedic approaches focus on the energy of the body. Different herbs are used to balance the body. The Chinese system attempts to balance Yin and Yang, the opposite types of energy within the body. If the body is too Yin, the herbalist balances it with Yang herbs and vice versa. There are also herbs to strengthen the life energy (chi) and cleanse and nourish the body. Western herbs focus more on the physical body. The herbs nourish and/or cleanse the body thereby strengthening its ability to heal.

Homeopathy - Homeopathy is a system of medicine which is nearly 200 years old. According to the law of similars, disease is cured by stimulating the body with an energy remedy. The remedy is derived from a substance which, if given in large doses, is capable of producing the same symptoms the patient is experiencing. For example, homeopathically prepared onion (allium cepa) may be given if a patient is experiencing tearing eyes,

watery, irritating discharge from the nose and a desire for fresh air. Most of you would recognize these symptoms as those produced when exposed to the vapors of cut onions. However, these symptoms may also occur in someone with hayfever. The cause is not important. How the individual responds is what counts. This results in individualized remedy selection based on the patient, NOT THE DISEASE. The treatment of arthritis in ten dogs may require a different remedy for each one.

These are only a few of the holistic alternatives available. Others include massage, Bach flower essences, bio-magnets, scent and color therapy. The practitioners of all of these systems recognize the individual as a whole body with a mind and spirit, not as a liver or kidney problem. They realize that only the individual can heal him or herself. However, the healing mechanisms must be allowed to operate unhindered. Holistic healing methods maximize healing functions and remove existing impediments.

Other varieties of holistic medicine include a balance between holistic and conventional medicine. First aid, basic health, nutritional balance, and basic remedies based on vitamins, minerals, trace elements and herbs are used to keep the dog healthy, improve his immune system and prevent common ailments before they develop. It is important to take the time to understand the process and to tailor it to your individual pet's needs.

BRINGING HOME A NEW DOG OR PUPPY

When you have selected your new dog, you need to get ready for its arrival. Decide who in the family is responsible for the care, feeding, exercise and discipline of the dog. Decide what rules the dog and the members of the family must live by. Dogs are very smart and will learn that different members of the family have different expectations. One member of the family may allow him on the bed, while another bedroom may be off limits entirely. Dogs adapt to a routine. They will expect that one member must arrive home before they can go on their walk. They may learn that when they see a certain pattern of behavior it means an outing which will include them, while another pattern of behavior means that the family will leave and they will stay at home. They will learn sounds of cars which belong in the family, and who is a regular visitor. They will learn where and how to go out to the bathroom, and when food will be provided. It is good to decide on a pattern of care before the dog or puppy arrives.

Our breeders related that Cocker Spaniels are good watch dogs. They will learn and bark differently when a family car arrives in the driveway and when it is a strange car. They will favor the person who cares for them, brushes them, and feeds them, especially if it is the same person who does all three. However, when the jobs are taken over by another person, they will switch favorites. Cockers do love to play and get human attention, and they will be loving toward the entire family if everyone is involved with them at some level.

If you purchase an older dog, be aware that although the dog may be housetrained in his old surroundings, it may take several days or even weeks to adjust to the new family and new surroundings. Let him have time to adjust before you overwhelm him. Be kind, yet firm in the rules. It is kinder to establish what you expect of him from the beginning than to let him adjust and then to impose rules once he has become comfortable. Remember, Cockers get their feelings hurt easily, so be firm and quiet, not loud or violent in your discipline. Once he adjusts, the older dog will be ready to join right in with the new family, to travel and visit and meet friends, to play with pre-teen or teenage children. He does not require as much time, training or care as a puppy.

Most of our breeders strongly recommended using a crate to housetrain, or to establish a pattern with either an older dog or a puppy. Contrary to some popular opinion, dogs love crates. A crate is their cave, or their home. Dogs, like their ancestors the fox, wolf and coyote, like the feeling of a "den," and the most successful doghouses are not huge structures, but small, enclosed areas that allow for "nesting." If you are buying a crate, be sure to get one big enough for the dog to live in as an adult, but not too big. One which is too large allows the puppy to soil it, and one which is too small is uncomfortable. Most breeders recommended what is commonly known as a #200 crate: ask your breeder for the exact size. Wire or plastic airline crates are both good.

Use the crate with common sense. Never leave a dog in a crate for excessive lengths of time, as Cockers need their exercise as much as their comfort. But crating not only helps housetrain, it also allows the owner to relax and enjoy himself without worrying about the dog, watching it to be sure it does not soil the carpet, or keeping an eye out to see if it is tearing up the house.

If you allow EITHER A NEW ADULT OR A PUPPY to have "accidents" in the house, you will have an even harder time breaking him of the habit later on. Never let him out of your sight until you are sure you can trust his judgment.

Dogs like the feeling of their own cave and using a crate will keep them from having accidents or causing damage when you are away from home.

Ask your breeder if the pup or dog is crate trained. Many breeders are believers in crates, and all show dogs must learn to travel and stay in crates at dog shows. If the dog is an older dog who has shown, he will probably be crate trained already. If the dog is not trained, put him in the crate and leave the room, staying near the door. He will probably sit there for a few minutes, then begin to cry, whine, scratch or bark. At the first noise, intervene with a sharp, "NO!" The dog or puppy will begin to associate the startling voice with his attempts to get out of the crate. Some of our breeders said they used a water pistol or spray bottle filled with clear water. When the dog or pup began to cry, they would shoot a sharp, short burst of water at the dog until he stopped. Repeating this several times with the word "NO!" seemed to make the point a little more strongly. They also suggested using a water gun when the dog was out of the crate to stop unwanted behavior in the house such as chewing or scratching at doors.

Once he is quiet in the crate for about thirty to forty-five minutes, praise him quietly. Don't make a big thing out of this. Cockers, especially young dogs, have a tendency to "leak" when excited. If your praise is too boisterous he is likely to get excited and urinate. Put him outside. Watch and see if he goes to the bathroom. If he does, praise him lavishly.

Bring him back in the house and let him play and be free for fifteen to twenty minutes. If he begins to chew something that is not a toy, take it away, say "No!" sharply, and replace the item with a toy. Cockers love toys and can easily be distracted with them. After play time, put him back in the crate and repeat the process. Consistency will help him learn housetraining through association. He should be crate trained after only a few short tries. The other things may take longer!

He should be able to keep the crate clean all night by the time he is three to four months old. The more careful you are with your routine, and the more consistent, the more rapidly he will train. Never give him more time to play and be free in the house than he can handle without having an accident. By the time he is five to six months old, he should be fairly well house trained. The fewer times he makes a mistake, the sooner he will be a reliable member of the family. Use common sense and don't leave him in the crate too much.

Puppies will need to eliminate shortly after eating, playing or waking. Do not play with him or excite a puppy who has just awakened, as this will cause him to leak. When he eliminates outside, always praise him. Puppies are like babies. A puppy will need time to grow up and he will take much more than a couple of weeks to be housetrained. He will chew, may dig, and will carry things around. It will take him a year to grow up and be mature. Like a baby, it simply takes him time to get rid of some of his exuberant puppy energy, learn manners, and behave like a companion should behave. Judgment on what is his and what is yours, how to please you, and how to use his energy will take time and maturity.

Traveling with a puppy takes a little more time and energy. To help prevent him from being carsick, don't feed or water him immediately before you leave. Many pups get car sick throw up or drool constantly in a moving car. Most of them outgrow it by the time they are six or seven months old.

Puppies are fun. It is a great temptation for friends and family members to overpower a puppy, exhaust him, and even lower his resistance. Give the pup time to get adjusted to his new environment. Do not allow friends and family to carry him around to the point of exhaustion.

If you have a dog already, be aware that your older dog may dominate your new puppy. Do not allow your new puppy to be kenneled or fed with an older dog. The puppy could be permanently ruined by a strong-willed dog. No matter how kind the older dog may seem, he may dominate the younger dog.

On the first night home, whether you have picked up the pup or had him flown in, be prepared that the pup will be lonely. It is likely that he has never been away from his littermates. He may be lonely when the lights turn out. He may cry or carry on. Be firm but understanding. Establish a routine from the beginning. Remember, it takes six hours for food to go through a dog. Feed him and walk or let him out for exercise on a regular basis. A puppy must be fed three or four times a day, depending on his age and established patterns. This can gradually be reduced to twice a day by the time he is six months old, and once for an adult. Regular exercise in the form of walks or playtime will also help regulate his system. Always let him out the last thing before you leave the house and the last thing at night. After a while he will get used to the routine and realize this is his last chance to go to the bathroom before having to spend time in his crate. This routine will help encourage him to eliminate and reduce the likelihood of soiling his crate.

Before you bring the new dog or puppy home, be prepared. Find out what the breeder is feeding and what the feeding schedule is. Get food and water bowls of appropriate size, and decide where to put them. Decide where the dog will sleep. If you are using a crate, be sure it will fit if it needs to stay up most of the time. It must be somewhere where it will not be in the way of the family. Once the Cocker is

Older dogs in the home may not be as excited about a new puppy as you are. Be careful not to allow them together without supervision.

housetrained, a bed or blanket may be good indoors. Outside, a box with shavings may be better. Remember, a Cocker is a retrieving breed, and a bored Cocker will almost certainly drag a blanket all over the yard, and may even reduce the large blanket to several small ones!

Toys or chew bones are good things to have on hand. The rawhide chew bones with a knot on the end were preferred by breeders over the flat chips which become soft and may choke a dog if swallowed. There are a number of good chew items on the market today, some of which may be ordered through the catalogue companies in the rear of the book in the section called the "Shopping Arcade."

Most of our breeders recommended against leaving a collar on a dog, especially a puppy. Small feet may get hung up in them, or they may become hooked on something in the house or yard. Put the collar on when you are taking him on the leash, and remove it before you leave him unattended, even in the crate.

One other interesting item you may want to have on hand is a "snood." While not necessary for puppies, you will need to introduce your dog to a snood as soon as possible so that he gets used to wearing it. Simply speaking, a snood is tube made out of cloth with elastic in each end. It fits around the top of his head and covers his ears, with the bottom elastic around the lower neck. If you will put this on before feeding, it will keep the ears out of the food bowl. This will keep the floor clean, and keep the ears from being covered with food when he eats. A raised food bowl also helps, both by keeping the ears clean, and by aiding digestion because the dog does not have to drop his head lower than his body in order to eat.

Arrange to pick up your dog or pup at a time when you will be home. Friday may be good, if you have time on the weekend to spend with him and help him get used to you as a new owner.

TRAINING A DOG YOU CAN LIVE WITH!

Good training and exercise seems to be the hardest thing for pet owners to understand and give their dogs. Our breeders recommended obedience classes. Cockers are very good in obedience work in the ring, but even if you never intend to show, obedience classes help you raise a well mannered dog you can live with. Early training is very important. Without it, a problem dog can develop and problem dogs are the ones who end up in the SPCA. No breeder wants to think of his or her puppy ending up in a rescue situation. Breeders said over and over again that proper socialization — that is, exposing the dog to strangers and a wide variety of situations as well as spending quality, loving time with him at home — was the biggest thing which would insure success. One breeder said that how long it took to housetrain and leash train, and whether a Cocker was neurotic as an adult, all depended on the consistency and care of early training and socialization. Time invested in a puppy is invaluable in producing a good dog, and lack of time invested as a puppy is very difficult to make up once the dog is an adult with bad habits or a neurotic personality.

Before you bring your dog home, plan a place for him in your home. Have a place for him to sleep, and food bowls for him to eat. Provide him with toys which are his to chew and brushes, nail clippers and perhaps even a snood so he can get used to these grooming tasks from the beginning. It is also important that you decide on the rules for the dog before he comes home to insure consistency from the beginning.

There are several good books on training. If there are no obedience classes in your area, buy one or two of these publications, or a video on the subject, and read or view it thoroughly. Puppies are cute and they often have behaviors which are cute in a puppy. But some of these behaviors are NOT cute in an adult. For example, a pup may stare at you, then if you hold his stare, snap at your face. This is funny with an uncoordinated puppy, but not funny at all in an adult dog. It is dangerous and unpleasant once the dog is grown. If you do not think the behavior is appropriate for an adult dog, DO NOT LET THE PUPPY BEGIN THE BEHAVIOR. Correct him sharply with a "NO" when he starts it. It is much harder to break bad habits than to establish the ground rules to begin with.

KEEP IN TOUCH WITH THE BREEDER

A good breeder's job does not stop when the puppy goes home. Call the breeder when you arrive home or when the dog arrives by plane to let him know that everything is fine. Call him in a few weeks and discuss any problems or rewarding experiences you have had with your new family member. Send a photo whenever you can. It helps breeders evaluate their breeding programs and most of them truly enjoy hearing news of their "children."

Playpens such as this one, or any one of several other types, are an excellent way to contain your dog when you are away from home. Playpens of several different types may be obtained through companies in the Shopping Arcade.

Sometimes, due to changes in lifestyle or family pattern, it becomes necessary to find a new home for the dog. If so, you should contact the breeder BEFORE you give the dog away to a new home or take him to the SPCA. Many breeders require this notice in their contracts, but we suggest that you make the effort to contact the breeder under such circumstances, whether or not it is mentioned in your contract. Good breeders are interested in their dogs, and they wish to follow them throughout their lifetime.

PAPERWORK

*T*he term "AKC registered" has meant, up until a few years ago, that a dog simply had a dam which carried AKC papers and a sire who carried AKC papers and they were both of the same breed. Any dog with two registered parents was eligible for registration, regardless of its quality.

In recent years, AKC has responded to pressure to put some limit to the number of breeding dogs in the general population. Since 1991, dogs may be marked by their original breeder as "non-breedable." This designation means that the dog will be issued papers from the AKC with a gold, rather than a purple border. If such an animal is bred, even if bred to a dog or bitch with a regular purple bordered certificate with full breeding privileges, the puppies produced will not be eligible for registration with AKC.

The registered name of a dog is often in two or three parts. The kennel name of the original breeder usually begins the name, followed by the name of the individual dog, and finally a second kennel name may follow if the dog was purchased as an unnamed puppy by another breeding kennel. This practice dates back to the early years in England when dogs were referred to by their owner's name first, because names in those days were very simple and duplication of names for dogs in the field was common. To make reference easier, people began to refer to the dogs as "Lord Grimstone's Susan," or "the Duke of Hamilton's Sam." These, combined with the year of their whelping, comprised the early pedigree records.

Today, a dog may be named, as with the bitch on page 82, "Ch. Green-Oaks Jerhico of Jemar." Nicknamed "Jerry," the name shows that the dog named "Jerhico" was bred by Eileen Chenevert of Green-Oaks Cockers — the Ch. before the name designates that he has earned his championship title — and was purchased as a puppy (before registration) by Mary Stacey of Jemar Cockers. Thus the dog is "Ch. (the championship title earned through dog shows) Green-Oaks (designating the breeder) Jerhico (the individual dog's name) of Jemar (owned by Mary Stacey).

Dogs bred and owned by a breeder at the time of registration will carry only one kennel name, usually in front of the individual dog's name. The dog on page 65, "Ch. Seacliffe's Sophistication," was bred by Herbert Kozuma of Seacliffe Cockers, and the individual dog's name is "Sophie," short for "Sophistication." She was still owned by Mr. Kozuma at the time of her registration, and was still owned by him at the time of printing.

As explained on page 63, dogs who compete successfully earn titles which stay with them throughout their lives. Only conformation championship titles precede the name.

Unless otherwise specified, "Ch." refers to an AKC title. Some dogs will have abbreviations of countries which indicate that they have earned conformation championships in more than one country. (Can., Am. Ch. - would be Canadian, American Champion.)

Other titles follow the name of the dog. These include field titles, obedience titles and other levels of achievement, including the latest AKC title of recognition — CGC — Canine Good Citizen. Learn more about titles in the section on competition.

When you buy a puppy, the breeder should give you a kennel pedigree. This will be a "tree" of names, like those in the "Hall of Fame" section. This lists the sire, dam, grandparents, and so on of the puppy. It will look something like this:

```
                                          grand sire of sire
                         sire of sire
                                          grand dam of sire
         sire
                                          grand sire of sire
                         dam of sire
                                          grand dam of sire
YOUR DOG
                                          grand sire of dam
                         sire of dam
                                          grand dam of dam
         dam
                                          grand sire of dam
                         dam of dam
                                          grand dam of dam
```

You should also receive either the AKC registration papers, or more likely, the "AKC DOG REGISTRATION APPLICATION" shown on the next page. The former is white, with a purple border; the latter is a blue form and must be submitted to AKC to receive the registration certificate. When you buy a puppy, it is possible that a breeder may not even have the dog registration applications for the litter back from AKC, especially if the puppy is very young. But you should get some kind of kennel pedigree, and at least a note, listing the sire, dam, and date of whelping to assure you the puppy is registered.

The BLUE litter registration will enable you to register your dog. Fill it out, including the name chosen for your dog in the boxes provided. Fill in the color and the back of the form and send it to AKC for your dog's registration. THIS IS NOT YOUR REGISTRATION - AND YOU ONLY HAVE <u>ONE YEAR</u> FROM THE <u>DATE THIS APPLICATION WAS ISSUED</u> TO BE ABLE TO REGISTER YOUR DOG!

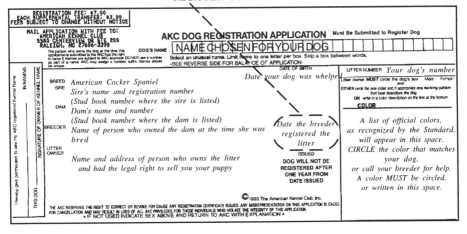

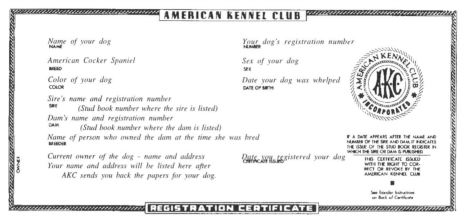

The AKC registration certificate for your dog will be issued when you fill out your blue puppy registration and submit it to AKC with the required fee, or, if you have an older dog, when you transfer your dog's registration to your name.

If the breeder has the dog registration applications — commonly called "puppy registrations," — back from AKC, they will be on blue paper. THIS IS NOT YOUR REGISTRATION CERTIFICATE. Be sure this blue form is filled out completely. Ask your breeder about naming your puppy. Some breeders insist that pups are named with a certain letter of the alphabet to help them track their pups throughout the years. Others will require that a word or idea is included in the name. Sometimes this can lead to funny and awkward names, especially if the letter is "X," "Y" or "Q"! Look to see which box is checked on the top of the form in regards to breedability of the dog. Be sure the breeder has signed as owner of the litter. Finally, be sure that "sex" and "color" are checked on the front of the puppy registration form.

ACCORDING TO AKC RULES which have only been in effect a few years, YOU MUST REGISTER THE DOG WITHIN ONE YEAR OF THE TIME THE PUPPY PAPERS HAVE BEEN ISSUED, or it cannot be registered. Therefore, it is important to take care of the paperwork as soon as possible.

Keep your kennel papers if you have them. If they were not provided, you can get a certified copy from AKC or use a pedigree service such as the one mentioned in the Shopping Arcade Section. Canine Family Tree will provide you with a complete pedigree, usually faster and less expensively than AKC. If you intend to breed your dog, you will most certainly need to know what is "behind" him or her. You will need to make inquiries about the strengths and weaknesses of these ancestors, and what will be most likely to match up with your pedigree to produce good quality puppies. If you intend to hire your male out for stud, bitch owners will ask to see a copy of the pedigree. If you wish to take your bitch to a stud for breeding, most stud owners will ask to see the pedigree before they agree to use their stud. They will want to look for lines with known health problems, and lines that will or will not match with those of their stud.

Even if you never intend to breed, it is worth the investment to send to a pedigree service

such as Canine Family Tree and get a copy. Champions of record will be marked in red, and it is a chance to see what famous dogs are in your dog's pedigree. You may enjoy matching the pedigree with those listed in the "Hall of Fame" section, looking for not only particular individuals, but familiar kennel names. When you receive your AKC registration certificate, it will NOT list the pedigree beyond the sire and dam of your dog. Send this information and their registration numbers (or simply send a photocopy of the registration certificate) to the pedigree service for the complete pedigree. The AKC registration is 8.5" X 4" with a purple border and the official AKC incorporation seal. It will also list the current owner and breeder.

If your dog is older and has already been registered, you will need to follow the "transfer instructions" on the back of the registration certificate. On the back, fill out Section A completely, be sure Section B has been signed and send in the fee and the ORIGINAL CERTIFICATE. AKC will issue a new certificate, with you listed on the front as the owner.

CARE

A Cocker Spaniel requires time and energy (and money) for grooming. An unkempt, unclipped Cocker Spaniel is a mass of knots and may even develop skin sores if the mats get too large or the skin becomes moist under the mats.

Early training should include brushing and combing a puppy. Several of our breeders also encourage new owners to get their puppies used to blow dryers. Introducing these things at an early age makes grooming easier.

Show grooming is extremely labor intensive. Breeders said it took them three to four hours to do a dog. All show grooming is done by hand, with no scissors or electric clippers. If you are going to enter your Cocker in a show, call the breeder or hire a handler for the first time. Do not take the dog to a commercial grooming salon for a show clip. Be aware that the American Cocker is a "Coated Breed." In show terms, this means that the look and condition of the coat have a lot to do with whether the dog wins or loses. Show coats take a lot of time to grow, and a lot of care to maintain. Therefore, the American Cocker is not a good breed if you want to show a dog once a month or a few times a year, and keep him as a pet during the rest of the time. Short coated breeds are much better suited for this type of dual purpose.

Pets will require a trip to the groomer every four to six weeks, depending on the clip and the hair of the dog. If your dog runs outside a good deal through grass or bushes, keep the clip short and easy to care for if grass, leaves and twigs become entangled in it. If your dog stays inside most of the time, and you like the look of a longer cut and don't mind the brushing, less frequent visits to the groomer will make a longer clip more appropriate.

Regular bathing is necessary. Use a good shampoo and a conditioner or detangler to make the hair comb out easier. Brushing and grooming will take approximately twenty minutes a day on average. This means a little more time on the day you bathe your dog, a little less if you have just washed him and brushed or combed him out the day before. And of course, if you are busy, you can skip a day. However, you can **not** average the coat care by taking one day a week and grooming the dog for two hours!

Mats build up rapidly without regular care, and once in, are time consuming to get out. Mats which are too bad will need to be cut out, and it doesn't take many of these "cut out" spots before your Cocker takes on a decidedly moth-eaten appearance! Our breeders generally agreed that grooming needed to be done *at least* every three to four days.

Remember too, that one thing that makes a Cocker a pet instead of a show dog is a "cottony" coat. Although they are still lovely to look at, they are harder to maintain and have more of a tendency to mat than a good show coat. As you can see from our Hall of Fame pictures, coats are very important to show breeders, so again, if you insist on your "pet" puppy having a superb, easy-to-care-for coat, expect to pay more because the trait you are looking for is the same trait the show breeder is looking for.

If you have decided to purchase a long-haired dog like a Cocker Spaniel, you need to accept the grooming. Many owners use this time as a way to relax after a long day at work and as a way to develop a close bond with their dogs. Cockers love to be pampered, especially if they have become used to it from the time they are young. This special time between you and your dog can be enjoyable for both parties and builds communication, trust and love. Cockers need mental care as well as physical care and this is an excellent way of providing a quiet setting to give that care instead of the excitement of play. It develops the quiet side of the dog and helps maintain a steady, less neurotic personality.

When you bathe your dog, it is best to apply eye ointment to protect the eyes from shampoo, and cotton soaked in alcohol to keep the water out of the ears. Use a good shampoo. There are a number of specialty soaps for long-coated breeds, some of which contain conditioners or detanglers. Try a number of different soaps until you find the one which is best for the coat on your dog. Remember that a puppy coat is much different than the coat of an adult dog and you may have to change shampoos after your dog is full grown and has an adult coat at about 1 1/2 years of age.

Be sure to rinse the coat well. Shampoo left in will wear out the hair and may cause itching. Use a blow dryer. Drying the coat keeps the dog from getting chilled, saves the house from water on the carpet or floors, and keeps the hair from matting during drying.

There are a number of products which are good to use between baths. One, called, "self-rinse," acts as a kind of cleaner for the hair. Another is "detangler," which helps get out knots before they become mats. Rinsing in vinegar and water is good for the coat, or use fresh lemon juice on buff colored dogs to keep the coat light in color, clean looking and smelling good.

It is very important to keep a check on the Cocker's ears. Like any long-eared dog, fungus infections may be a problem, especially in humid climates. Keep a check on ear wax and sniff regularly for odor. The odor of an ear infection is very distinctive and easy to recognize even if you have never smelled it before. If you have *any* fleas in the area, you may also have an ear problem. Fleas and ear mites love the dark, moist areas of the long eared dog. Lift up the ear and look at the ear canal. If black "dirt" is evident at the edge of the ear canal, you should be sure it is treated. Another indication that your Cocker has an ear problem is if he shakes his head or carries it cocked to one side when he walks. There are a number of different products available, both over the counter and from your vet, to control these problems. Most of our breeders recommended that you take the dog to the vet if you see black "dirt" or smell an odor in the ear. Ask your vet how to treat the particular problem. Usually you will be able to treat future problems at home once you have learned the symptoms to look for and what to do about it, though treatment can sometimes be lengthy and the condition difficult to completely eliminate. Prevention through regular cleaning with alcohol and cotton swabs at the time you do your regular grooming is the best course of action.

Keep the area under the eyes wiped clean. There are several cosmetic products available through catalogue companies that will clean the discoloration, which is more noticeable on a light coated dog than on a black or dark colored dog. If the eye is excessively runny or matted, consult your veterinarian. Otherwise, wipe the eye area when you bath and groom your dog.

A number of breeders mention care of the flews. Flews, that area on each side of the jaw that hangs down from the muzzle and overlaps the lower jaw, are loose in the Cocker Spaniel. Be aware that food particles may collect in those folds of the mouth on the outside of the cheek. If not cleaned on a regular basis, an infection may start. This infection has a noticeable odor. One breeder recommended using Listerine to wipe out the area. Other breeders felt that this was not generally a problem if the dog was in good health and on a correct diet. They felt there was no reason to worry about the flews unless the dog seemed to have a problem in that area.

Finally, feet of the Cocker need care. Keep the hair which grows down between the toes clipped, especially if the climate is snowy or muddy. Originally, sporting dogs grew hair between their pads to help protect their feet when traveling all day over rough terrain. Or, if the dog was out in snow, the hair was insulation against the cold. If your dog is basically a house pet, the hair is nothing more than a nuisance which will collect balls of ice in the winter on trips outside, and balls of mud in the spring! When the dog comes in, these balls are uncomfortable, so he lies down and proceeds to groom himself by pulling the mud or ice off the hair so that he can once again walk without feeling like he has a rock in his shoe. However, since the dog is not good at picking up the leftover mess and depositing it in the trash, it will be left in lumps of melting ice or dirt all over your floor. It is easier to take a pair of scissors, carefully pull the pads apart, and trim the hair between the pads. Get the puppy used to this early, and he will stand quietly for it by the time he is an adult.

Nails will wear down with exercise if the dog is outside and working hard, but today's companion and show dogs often have nails which grow until they are long enough to reach the floor, splay the feet, and cause discomfort when the dog walks or stands. Begin early to get the puppy used to nail clipping or grinding. In light colored nails it is easy see the

Lots of love is the key to a Cocker's well being and happiness.

"quick," or part of the nail which carries the blood supply, but the quick is almost impossible to detect in black nails. Cutting into the quick will cause bleeding. Although the nail may bleed profusely, this bleeding is simple to stop using blood stop or even flour which is readily available around the home. Another advantage of flour is that if the Cocker licks the nail, the flour will not hurt him.

Many of our breeders preferred grinding nails. Grinding may be done by special dog nail grinders, or you can go to the hardware store and buy a small hand grinder. Grinding is slower, but the heat from the grinder cauterizes the nail as it grinds, keeping the nail from bleeding. If you begin a puppy early, he will be used to the grinder by the time he is an adult.

Finally, light colored Cockers such as buffs or parti-colored dogs with white beneath their eyes, may develop tear stains under the eye. Although this condition does not affect the health of the dog, some owners consider it unsightly. There are a number of commercial products available through pet shops, grooming salons, or through mail order catalogues which do a good job removing the stains from the hair under the eye.

Tear stains are not an indication of eye problems, but may be unsightly to the owner. They may be removed with one of several non-prescription products available on the market.

FEEDING

Remember that feeding a dog is like feeding a baby. There are dozens of schools of thought, and thousands of dollars spent by dog food companies to develop, research and market their food. These high quality foods are complete and do not need to be supplemented with vitamins and other nutrients as they have already been formulated and balanced to the needs of dogs. Today, there are even a wide variety of foods for puppies, active adults, non-active adult dogs and old dogs.

Many of our breeders recommended dry dog food because it gives the puppy a chance to chew and strengthen his teeth. This chewing will help take the place of shoes and corners of cabinets and save some of your sanity. One breeder said that giving the dog a large soup bone, as can be found at a butcher shop or in many grocery store meat departments, will help keep the teeth clean and strong, and will give the dog hours of enjoyment.

We suggest you talk to your breeder about feeding. There are a number of good dog foods on the market. Find out what your dog has been used to eating. Dogs like a steady diet of the same thing, not a wide variety as cats and humans prefer. A puppy should eat three to four times a day, gradually decreasing the feedings to two by the time he is six months old, and adult dogs need to eat only once a day.

If there is no other dog in the house, you may want to "free feed," that is, put down a bowl of dry dog food and leave it down for the dog to eat when he pleases. Breeders who do that swear by it, claiming that there are actually LESS weight problems because the dog does not learn to gobble food when it is put down, knowing that there will be no more until the next day. The free fed dog eats his fill but no more, knowing that the food will always be there. Other breeders felt this was a very bad idea. They say that it is harder to housetrain a dog who eats at different times and in different amounts each day. They felt Cockers were prone to overeat and pointed out that overweight problems are common in older companion Cockers.

In the chapter on bringing home your dog, we suggested you get a "snood." Most of our breeders indicated that snoods were valuable for the cleanliness of the dog and the well being of the floor and walls. A Cocker has lovely, long ears, trimmed in hair. But when he puts his nose in the food bowl, the ears also go in the food bowl. With dry food that is not a problem, but with wet or canned foods, the ears can be covered with food by the time the meal is over. Water bowls are also a problem, leading to soaking wet ears with every drink. Snoods are easy to make, or may be purchased from one of the catalog companies. Show breeders would not be without them, and many pet owners find them a nice way to keep the house and floors clean during mealtime. Simply find some cotton or lightweight material you like, measure the widest part of the dog's head so it will pull over easily, and sew the fabric into a tube. Fold it over, put elastic in each end, and you have your own personal snood! The trick is to measure the widest part of the head, not the neck. This ensures it will be big enough to put on. The top part goes in front of the ears, and the bottom elastic goes around the lower part of the neck. Don't make the elastic too loose or it will come off, but don't make the bottom too tight or it will choke the dog. Another solution is to use a clothes pin or plastic clip and "pin" the ears up behind the dog's head. However, dogs frequently object to this method and must be acclimatized to the clip on their ear leathers which is sometimes more difficult than using the snood.

Because Cockers are people dogs, they will eat whatever they see humans enjoying. One breeder sent an article and asked that we remind our readers that chocolate is very

bad for dogs, and can kill them in sufficient quantities. Cockers are small dogs, so the quantity required to make them sick is fairly small. As little as a pound may be harmful, and even less for a puppy. If you have small children, be sure they do not leave candy in reach of the dog, and do not let them share their treat with the dog. Be sure to impress on them that although this is a treat for them, it can be very harmful to the Cocker.

Safety-proof your home for your dog, just as you would for a small child, you should: 1) Fence your yard or be sure the dog is walked on a leash, not turned loose out the front or back door. 2) Keep drawers and closets shut for pet safety and protection of personal articles. 3) Keep electrical and phone cords up where they cannot be chewed. 4) Pick up pins, tacks, marbles, bottle caps and other small objects which can be swallowed. 5) Never leave chocolate within reach of the dog. Many dogs love it and will make of point of helping themselves. 6) Store medicine, cleaning supplies and insecticides in closets with doors that can be closed securely. 7) Keep fireplace screens in place at all times. 8) Do not allow moist dog food to sit out all day at room temperature. It will spoil and can make the dog sick if he comes back to eat it.

Dry dog foods may be left out and within reach of the dog. 9) Keep garbage lids tightly closed to avoid possible digestive disturbances and nuisance problems. 10) Never tie ribbons around the neck of pets. They can get caught and pulled too tight. 11) Keep car products such as antifreeze and motor oil away from the dog. Do not allow the dog to "help" you if you are working with such products. 12) If you are working on the car on a hot day, don't let the dog outside with you. Dogs may jump unnoticed into the car if the door is open, and the owner may fail to notice the sleeping dog when he closes the door and goes in the house, leaving the dog in the hot car to suffer heat stroke.

13) NEVER LEAVE YOUR DOG IN THE CAR ON A HOT DAY. 14) Don't let the postman hand mail to your child if the dog is present. Cockers are protective of their families, especially children, and may interpret the mailman as a threat. 15) Keep chairs pushed up to the table. This prevents the dog from using the chair to get on to the table where he may be injured or cause damage.

DOG SHOWS
AND OTHER COMPETITIONS

Many a dog has lived his entire life as a companion, a friend, and a confidant to his family without ever finding the need to have a career of his own. But some dogs do work for a living, and if they prove worthy, will earn a degree or title to attach to their names. The most common of these is a "Conformation" title from AKC. As you can see from our Hall of Fame section, dogs of outstanding quality and attitude are referred to as "Champion." The title Ch. appears before their registered name, and is used every time the registered name is printed. Once earned, this title, like all dog titles, will stay with the dog for the rest of his life. A champion is a champion for life.

Championships are earned by exhibiting at AKC shows and collecting points. The number of points earned at each show will vary, depending on the number of dogs of that breed which are entered in competition and defeated. It takes 15 points for a dog to be a champion, but at least twice in his life the dog must take a "Major," that is he must earn three points at one show. This is not as easy as it might seem since there are not many majors a year, and the dog must win the top award in heavy competition.

American Cockers are divided into three "Varieties" in AKC competition. Points are awarded in each variety. Blacks show only against other blacks and black dogs with tan markings such as the one on page 71. Parti-colored dogs (those with a patched coloring such as the one on page 68) may be any color in their spotting, on a white background. ASCOB dogs are Any Solid Color Other than Black. Buff dogs such as "Ch. Gallant Molly Pitcher" on page 70 would show in this variety. Liver colored dogs or reds would also show in this variety.

Points are awarded for each breed based on how many dogs are showing in the area each year. There are nine AKC a divisions across the country and the points may be different for each division, and will be different for each sex and for each breed, and in Cockers, for each variety. For example, the chart on the next page shows the points needed for four of the nine AKC divisions in 1994. The location is the general area of the country. The North East includes: Connecticut, Maine, Massachusetts, New Hampshire, New York, Rhode Island and Vermont; the Midwest includes: Iowa, Kansas, Minnesota, Missouri, Nebraska and Wisconsin; and of course California and Alaska are just those states.

The points refer to the number of points earned if a given number of dogs or bitches are showing. For example, if you had a black dog winning at a show held in Maine, and five dogs (including yours) showed that day, you would earn two points toward your dog's championship. But if you had a black bitch at the same show and five bitches (including yours) showed that day, you would only earn one point if she won, because six bitches are needed to earn two points in that area. The area of the country were the show is held is the deciding factor, not the home of the dog. Thus, owners of dogs traveling from one area of the country to another will need keep in mind the different point scales when computing their points. Points from all areas may be added together to earn a championship title.

No matter how many entries are attending a show, five points are the most that will be earned. Even if the show is a large "Specialty" (a show with which has been

Location	Variety	Points	Dogs	Bitches	Location	Variety	Points	Dogs	Bitches
Northeast:	Black	1	2	2	California:	Black	1	2	2
		2	4	6			2	6	8
		3	7	10			3	10	14
		5	15	20			5	20	28
	ASCOB	1	2	2		ASCOB	1	2	2
		2	5	7			2	6	6
		3	9	13			3	10	11
		5	15	23			5	19	20
	Parti	1	2	2		Parti	1	2	2
		2	5	5			2	7	7
		3	8	9			3	12	13
		5	14	17			5	23	27
Midwest:	Black	1	2	2	Alaska:	Black	1	2	2
		2	6	7			2	3	3
		3	10	13			3	4	4
		5	17	22			5	6	6
	ASCOB	1	2	2		ASCOB	1	2	2
		2	6	6			2	3	3
		3	10	11			3	4	4
		5	17	22			5	6	6
	Parti	1	2	2		Parti	1	2	2
		2	5	6			2	3	5
		3	9	11			3	5	9
		5	15	19			5	9	13

recognized by a regional or national American Cocker Club and attracts hundreds and hundreds of entries) it will still award only five points, but as you can see from our Hall of Fame, winning at a Specialty Show is considered more prestigious simply because of the larger number of entries.

Breeds with smaller numbers of dogs, or breeds with fewer dogs showing, will have very different numbers. Portuguese Water Dogs, a relatively unknown breed, showing at the same show in the same year would only need two dogs or bitches for a point, four dogs or bitches for two points, six dogs or bitches for three points, and ten dogs and nine bitches for five points! This is because there are far fewer Portuguese Water Dogs whelped and shown than there are American Cocker Spaniels. If the breed becomes popular and more dogs are shown, the points will begin to go up each year as the number of entries rises in shows in the area. When the number of entries in a breed falls, the points will go down the following year. In this way, AKC limits the number of champions in each breed or variety to about 150 to 200 per year. A listing of points in the area can be found in the show catalogue for each breed entered at the show, or you can call AKC Event Records Department. The new point system is printed each year in April and goes out with the AKC Calendar of Events, a monthly publication listing shows across the country for the next several months.

As you may have noticed from the point system, in the world of dog shows, a "dog" is a male and only a male, and a female is a "bitch." Classes in dog shows are divided by dogs and bitches. The top winning dog will be "Winners Dog," and the top winning female will be named "Winners Bitch." The best between them is the "Best of Winners"

In conformation competition, all entries for a class enter the ring at the same time. The judge looks at the entire class, standing, from the side and moving around the ring at the trot. The judge then "goes over" each entry, that is to say, he looks at the teeth and puts his hands on each dog to feel the structure. Each entry is then moved at the trot and the judge looks at the movement as the dog goes away, from the side, and as the dog returns to the judge. While in the ring, dogs are to stand at attention at all times and to behave with manners toward their handlers, the judge, and other dogs.

Black dogs show as a separate variety.

To attend a show, call your local kennel club, watch the newspapers, look in the phone book which often lists yearly events in the area and will sometimes list the dog shows, call the AKC Event Records Office, or call your breeder. Once you are at a show, visit the vendors around the grounds. Those selling general merchandise will usually sell calendars with the shows listed on them. Some of our vendors in the Shopping Arcade also carry these calendars.

If you have never entered a dog in a show, perhaps the best thing to do is go and see what a show is like. Entries must be made two and a half weeks ahead of time, and a program is printed for each show, listing each dog entered, its name, owner, breeder and age. Dogs will show first. Puppy dogs, Novice dogs, Bred by Exhibitor dogs (those whose breeders are actually showing them, American Bred dogs (open to any dog bred in the United States) and Open dog. The first place winners from each class will go back into the ring to pick Winners Dog. Then the bitches show, through the same classes, and the first place winners will return for Winners Bitch. Only the Winners Dog and Winners Bitch will win points — all other dogs and bitches will go home empty handed!!!

For that reason, people often hire handlers. These professionals know how to present a dog to its best advantage, and they know the judges and what certain judges are looking for in a dog. Sometimes owners will show their own dogs, and that is referred to as "owner handled." You may see that term in our Hall of Fame section. Sometimes a dog will even travel with the handler to the show and the owner does not attend at all. If your breeder sold you your dog with a contract which says he must be shown, you may be required to send the dog with a handler in order to get him "finished," that is, to earn his championship.

Once a dog has earned his title, he will show only in the "Best of Breed" class. Champions and the Winner's Dog and Winner's Bitch for the day will return to the ring to select the "Best of Breed." If the Best of Breed is a dog, a bitch will be chosen as "Best of Opposite Sex." If the Best of Breed is a bitch, a dog will be named Best of Opposite Sex. Only the Best of Breed will return to the group ring at the end of the day to compete in the "Group."

All breeds are divided into one of seven Groups: Sporting, Non-Sporting, Herding, Working, Terriers, Toys and Hounds. There are about fifteen to twenty breeds in each group. The winner of each group will return to the Best in Show ring where the final seven dogs compete to be named the "Best in the Show." You may have watched parts of the Group judging or Best in Show judging from Madison Square Garden on cable television. Other famous local shows are sometimes broadcast.

In the early days of showing, in the 1930's, all champions were in the Open Class and "Specials Only" meant your dog was for sale or on exhibition. Almost all shows were benched, with dogs tethered with chains. There were raised platforms in the middle of the ring which the judges used to compare exhibits, and the winner was always placed "On the Block." Most of the exhibitors were people of wealth and social position and owners seldom showed their own dogs.

Westminster was a three day affair offering benching. Colored cards in place of ribbons were displayed on the back of each dog's bench to help the public recognize the winners. Kennel men often spent the night on the benches with the dogs.

Today, the average AKC show will have about 1,000 to 1,500 dogs entered. Some will have entries of 2,500 to 3,500. One show in Louisville, Kentucky, has reached 5,000 entries! There is a lot of excitement at a show, and usually ten to twenty-five rings are being judged at once. If you do not have the judging schedule ahead of time and wish to be sure to see a certain breed, be sure to arrive about 8:30 in the morning. Some shows start as early as 8:00, and each breed is judged at a certain pre-scheduled time in a specific ring. A judging schedule is available ahead of time to exhibitors, and generally arrives in the mail about three to four days before the show. If you arrive too late, you may find that the breed you are interested in has already been judged early in the morning, and only the Best of Breed dog is still on the grounds. Or, the dogs may be back at their vans and cars, scattered across a large parking lot and almost impossible to find. We have very few classic Bench Shows left in this country, so dogs are not on exhibit all day. They are brought up from their cars and vans, shown, and returned to rest until their owners are ready to go home.

Buff is the most common color showing in the Any Solid Color Other than Black (ASCOB) variety. Liver and red are other solid colors which would also show in this variety.

Obedience is another event at most dog shows. Unlike conformation showing where no special training is needed to start showing a young dog, obedience dogs are required to show off lead and through a specific set of exercises. Judging is very precise. Scoring is done by subtracting points for faults such as failing to sit square, to return fully, or to stay in step on the heel exercise. Conformation dogs do not need to sit — in fact they should NOT sit while in the ring. Obedience dogs are required to sit when the handler stops walking, and when a command is given throughout the exercise program.

Obedience dogs need to have reached a level of training where they can go through precise movements on the command of their handlers, including heel, sit, stay and down. An obedience dog must be by nature intelligent and be willing to please. Although not always

During the class, the dog is required to move around the ring at the trot. Cockers have a characteristic movement which is very stylish and flashy.

excited about keeping their mind on the task at hand, there have been a number of Obedience Titled Cockers. These dogs have, through diligent work with their owners, become talented obedience dogs. "Princess Margaret," on page 83, is an example of a talented obedience dog. On page 6, Ch. Shalimar's Regal Challenge, CDX, is shown participating in an advanced level obedience class, going over a jump in full show coat.

Conformation classes and obedience classes are held at the same time, so it very difficult, especially for a young dog and a novice handler, to adapt to the different types of showing and work with the conflicting schedules which often develops.

Dogs begin with the Novice class. A and B divisions relate to the handler. "A" dogs are handled by their owners, and only one dog may be shown in the class, while a "B" dog may be handled by a professional handler or trainer, and several dogs may be handled by the same owner or handler in the same class.

There are six exercises which score points. These are: Heel on Leash, Stand for Examination, Heel Free, Recall, Long Sit, and Long Down, with a possible total of 200 points. All but the Heel on Leash must be done off lead, and a dog must score at least 50% of the available points in each exercise AND have a total score of 170 or higher in three obedience trials (with at least six dogs in competition) to earn the title of C.D. (Companion Dog) Once the C.D. is earned, the dog moves up to the next level.

This level has seven exercises. Each must be precisely executed. They are: Heel Free, Drop on Recall, Retrieve on Flat, Retrieve Over High Jump, Broad Jump, Long Sit, and Long Down. Three qualifying scores at three different shows are needed to earn the title of C.D.X. Dogs may then move up to Utility Dog competition to earn a U.D. title. This is the highest title an obedience dog can earn. The seven exercises include scent discrimination, hand signals, and both broad and high jumps.

Almost any show has classes for obedience. They are usually held in a ring apart from the conformation showing. If you are interested in showing your dog in obedience, begin with a local obedience class. Be prepared to work with him on a daily basis for several

(cont. p. 97)

HALL

OF

FAME

THE FOLLOWING SECTION IS A SHOWCASE FOR STARS OF THE BREED.
        All of the dogs pictured on the following pages are title holders. These animals will give you an idea of what current outstanding individuals of the breed look like and what bloodlines produce these qualities. The breeders and kennels listed on these pages represent the range of styles within the breed. Look closely at the dogs, the pedigrees and what each breeder has to say. If you already own an American Cocker Spaniel, see if your dog looks like any of the dogs on the following pages, or if they share any of the same ancestors.
        We congratulate the breeders and owners of these dogs for their dedication to fine American Cocker Spaniels. Their time and effort insures not only the success of their dogs, but the continuation of the breed.

Here is an explanation of some of the titles you will see:

Ch. - (Champion) — This conformation title precedes the name and unless otherwise indicated, denotes the American Kennel Club (AKC) title. Abbreviations of countries before Ch. indicate that the dog is a champion of record for each of the countries listed. In that case, Am. would be listed for an American Champion so that it is clear the dog has earned his AKC title as well as those issued by other countries.

Other titles will follow the name of the dog:

CD - Companion Dog, an obedience title.
CDX - Companion Dog Excellent, the next level of obedience.
UD - Utility Dog, the highest level of obedience title.
TT - Temperament Tested.
CGC - Canine Good Citizen, a title awarded by AKC through a specific test of obedience and temperament.

Please note that minor discrepancies in the presentation of titles is a result of breeder preference and the lack of a universal protocol.

FRONT COVER DOG:

Ch. Dur-Bet's Pick The Tiger
Ch. Windy Hill's Tis Demi's Demon
Ch. Windy Hill's Tis Demi-Tasse
Ch. Must-Do's Matador
Ch. Shoestring Shootin' Match
Must-Do's Magic Moment
Ch. Kaplar's Kap-T-Vator
Ch. Regal's Tribute To Matador
Ch. Palm Hill Caro-Bu's Solid Gold
Ch. Palm Hill's Krugerand
Palm Hill's Luv Thy Neighbor
Ch. Beaujolais Snapdragon
Ch. Cottonwood Congressman
Palm Hill's Starlett O'Hara
Ch. Palm Hill's Tiger Lily

Mitchell is one of 5 BIS dogs bred and owned by Regal Cockers. He is one of 85 homebred champions finished by the Pecks along with 17 other Champions the Pecks bought and finished during the 14 years of showing and 12 years of breeding. The Pecks were top breeders 3 times during this period and in the top 5 two other times. Mitchell is a perfect example of our standard. He is correct size, has a correct topline and tailset, scissor bite, beautiful neck and shoulders, perfect coat texture and tons of attitude. A product of two top producing lines, he is SLT/PRA clear and OFA. Stud fee: on request. Mitchell shown pictured with PHA Handler Ron Buxton.

Pat & Betty Peck
20475 Hayes Rd
Long Beach, MS 39560

Regal   Cockers
(601) 864-9450

BACK COVER DOG:

Ch. Durbet's Pick the Tiger
Ch. Windy Hill's Tis Demi's Demon
Ch. Windy Hill's Tis Demi Tasse
Ch. Must-Do Matador
Ch. Shoestring Shootin' Match
Must-do Magic Moment
Ch. Kaplar's Kap-T-Vator
Ch. Cashmere's Amazing Grace
Ch. Frandee's Forgery
Ch. Camelot's Countfeit
Ch. Camelot's Counterfeit
Tamra's All That Glitters
Ch. Frandee's Top Brass
Ch. Tamra's Wild Fire's Raging
Wild Fire's Frivolous Freea

American Spaniel Club- Best in Futurity
American Spaniel Club- Best of Breed
All Breed Best in Show
Specialty Best in Show
1991's Number One Bitch

What more do we need to say?

Debbie Bertrand & John Zolezzi
Eighty-Eights
Rt. 1, Box 405
Fresno, Texas 77545
(713) 980-9404 * (713) 431-1502 * (619) 436-1256

Bred by and Co-owned by
Lynn McLoughlin

CH. SEACLIFFE'S SOPHISTICATION

CH. ARTRU ACTION
CH. PINER'S PREMEDITATED
CH. RINKY DINK'S PINER'S EVERLUVIN'
CH. RINKY DINK'S BIT OF ACTION
CH. ARTRU SKYJACK
CH. LANEL'S RINKY DINK'S M &M
CH. RINKY DINK'S LANEL'S CINNAMON
CH. SEACLIFFE'S SOPHISTICATION
CH. ARTRU ACTION
SARCHELL'S BIG DADDY
SARCHELL'S SWEET MUSIC
CARLEN'S LOVE ME DEERLY
CH. ARTRU SKYJACK
PRIME-TIME SKYE'S THE LIMIT
DONN CARM'S RUNNING DEER

"Sophie" was one of three in her litter to finish. She attained her championship in relatively short order as did her littermates. She is the dam of five champions in very limited breedings and one litter of three finished their championships in major competitions. She is an ideal Cocker, merry, sound and a terrific temperament!

Herbert K. Kozuma
7395 W. Severence Lane
Las Vegas, Nevada 89131-3326

Seacliffe Cockers
(702) 658-7572

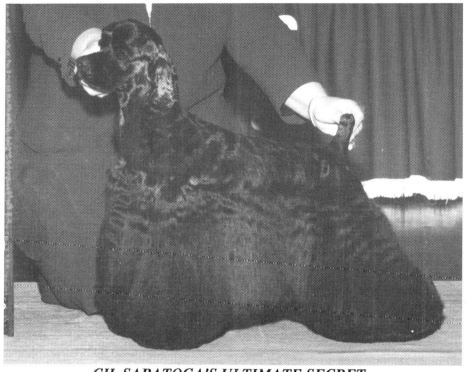

CH. SARATOGA'S ULTIMATE SECRET

CH. WINDY HILL'S TIS' DEMI'S DEMON
CH. MUST-DO'S MATADOR
MUST-DO'S MAGIC MOMENT
CH. REGAL'S SALUTE TO THE CLOWN
CH. RINKY DINK'S SIR LANCELOT
CH. REGAL'S SENT IN THE CLOWN
CH. HARRAN'S APRIL MISTY MORNIN
CH. SARATOGA'S ULTIMATE SECRET
CH. LIPTON'S CRUISIN' FOR A BRUISIN'
CH. SARATOGA'S PARTIAL ECLIPSE
TYPAM COUNTRY BUMPKIN
CH. SARATOGA'S SECRET CENTER
CH. WIL-CO'S WAR PAINT
SARATOGA'S EBONY AND IVORY
SARATOGA'S JIMINY CRICKETT

"Timmy" won an Award of Merit at the American Spaniel Club in both Jan. and July 1994. He has multiple Group Placements and multiple variety wins at Specialty and All Breed shows. He was the #2 black Cocker in the breed system for several months and continues his winning ways with elegance of movement, rock hard back and strong driving rear. He has a long neck and proper shoulder lay back for correct front reach. SLT/PRA clear 3/94 OFA certified. Saratoga Cockers has been breeding 12 years, producing 24 champions. "Timmy" is #14 champion for his dam, Ch. Saratoga's Secret Center ("Jesse"), who is the Top Producing black bitch in breed history.

Owner: Anne T. Coleman
Coleman Cockers
1457 Woodridge Rd
Marion, Ohio 43302
(614) 389-1457

Breeders: Joan and Tony Stallard
Saratoga Cockers
2562 Eden East
Northwood, Ohio 43619
(419) 691-1618

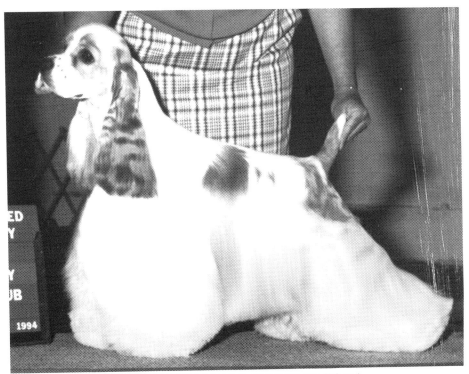

CH. COLEMAN'S SCOTCH N' SODA

```
                                    CH. GING'S ALYDAR
                        CH. TAGALONG'S MACHO MAN
                                    TLC TANNER'S CINNAMON SUGAR
            AM CAN CH. TAGALONG'S SHADYHILL STORM
                                    FRANDEE'S TRIUMPH
                        FRANDEE'S MS TAGALONG
                                    FRANDEE'S POTPOURRI
CH. COLEMAN'S SCOTCH N' SODA
                                    HOMESTEAD'S HAPPY CAMPER
                        CH. FAR-ACE JPK PRETTY BOY FLOYD
                                    SPINLER'S N J-DON'S PRESTIGE
            CH. JPK'S BEWITCHING
                                    CH. MY-IDA-HO DIAMOND JIM
                        FAR-ACE N JPK DANCIN' TIL DAWN
                                    J-DON'S FAR-ACE MAD MONEY
```

Coleman Cockers has been showing and breeding for show since 1989. With 10 homebred champions and over 20 champions finished all together, they are proud of Ch. Coleman's Scotch N' Soda - "Cutty." This red and white is eye catching with gorgeous coat and proper movement. He carries a hard back and has a long neck with proper shoulder layback. His disposition and excellent temperament make him a favorite of the kennel. SLT/PRA clear 2/94.

T. W. & Anne T. Coleman
1457 Woodridge Rd
Marion, Ohio 43302

Coleman Cockers
(614) 389-1457

CH. SWEETBRIAR'S BLACK EYED PEA

```
                                              CH. BALIWICK BARRYMORE
                              DERBY'S DANISH DEFENDER
                                              CH. DERBY'S DANISH DELIGHT
              CH. DERBY'S DEAL ME ACES
                                              CH HOMESTEAD'S RAGTIME COWBOY
                              DERBY'S DEVASTATING
                                              CH. DERBY'S DOUBLE DUTCH
CH. SWEETBRIAR'S BLACK EYED PEA
                                              CH. HOMESTEAD'S HUCKLEBERRY
                              CH. HOMESTEAD'S I'M SUM BUDDY
                                              CH. HOMESTEAD'S BUTTER BRICKLE
              CH. SAN JO'S SWEETBRIAR
                                              CH. TERJE'S THUNDERBOLT
                              SAN JO'S SPRING SHOWERS
                                              SAN JO'S DOTTIE DESIGN
```

"Drew" finished very quickly with several Best of Varieties. She is from a beautiful winning and producing pedigree. Her first litter by Ch. Shalimar's In Command will be making their debut in 1995.

Brenda (Rickenbacker) Hamm
106 Magnolia Dr
Greeneville, Tennessee 37743

Sweetbriar
(423) 638-1714

BEST IN
SHOW
AMERICAN
SPANIEL CLUB
1987
ASHBEY

AM/MEX CH. FRANDEE'S FORGERY

```
                                    CH. LUROLA'S ROYAL LANCER
                        CH. CHESS KING'S BOARD BOSS
                                    CH. RINKY DINK'S SERENDIPITY
            CH. FRANDEE'S FEDERAL AGENT
                                    CH. LUROLA'S SIR LAWRENCE
                        CH. FRANDEE'S PRIM N' PROPER
                                    CH. MAR-JAC'S FRANDEE FOLLY
CH. FRANDEE'S FORGERY
                                    CH. SANSTAR'S PIED PIPER
                        CH. FEINLYNE'S FOREMOST
                                    CH. FEINLYNE MINERVA
            CH. FEINLYNE FETCH AND GO
                                    CH. LUROLA'S ROYAL LANCER
                        FEINLYNE'S B T
                                    FEINLYNE'S FAIREST OF ALL
```

Forgery has had a great impact on the American Cocker in the last 10 years. At five years old he won Best in Show at the American Spaniel Club Show in January 1987 with his handler Diana Kane. Forge's greatest contribution to the breed has been his ability to consistently produce good sound Cockers. To date he has sired 55 champions, two American Spaniel Club Best of Breed Winners, multiple All Breed Best in Show winners and Group winners. His grandchildren are now repeating that same winning record. Forge is a special Cocker to the breed and also a good friend.

John Zolezzi   Searidge Cockers
568 Rancho Santa Fe Rd   (619) 436-1256
Olivenhair, California 92024

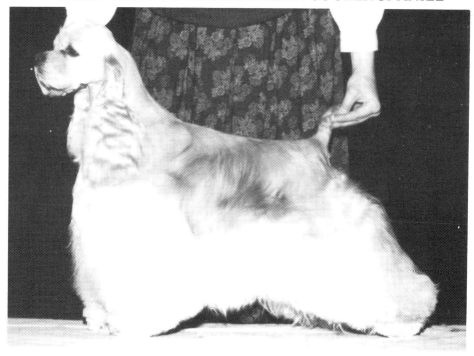

CH. GALLANT MOLLY PITCHER

```
                              CH. SHAM-O-JETS EAGER BEAVER
                    CH. SHAM-O-JETS BUCKY BEAVER
                              WESTWIND'S ANNIE'S SONG
          CH. GAZON CLEARLY DARKEHAVEN
                              CH. HARLANHAVEN HIGH SPIRIT
                    CH. SHAM-O-JETS REMEMBER ME
                              CH. SHAM-O-JETS ENCHANTING JILL
CH. GALLANT MOLLY PITCHER
                              CH. COTTONWOOD CONGRESSMAN
                    CH. PALM HILL CARO BU'S SOLID GOLD
                              CH. PALM HILL TIGER LILY, CD
          GALLANT VEGAS GIRL
                              CH. COMAC GOLDEN GAMBLER
                    CH. COMAC CASINO ROYALE
                              SUNSHINE SERANADE TO COMAC
```

Ch. Gallant Molly Pitcher received her championship when she was one day over 1 year old. In her first time out as a champion she went Group 1. She was # 3 bitch in the US in 1992 and # 7 ASCOB. She produced champion Gallant Eleanor R who finished going Best of Variety over specials. Because of Eleanor R, Molly is now the grandmother of a group winner. Her second litter produced Ch. Gallant Polar Express, a beautiful silver dog doing top winning. Her third litter looks very promising. But most importantly, she loves life, loves people and keeps us laughing.

Nancy and Tom Gallant
13991 P. Dr. N
Marshall, Michigan 49068

Gallant Country Cockers
(616) 781-5712

CH. CIN-DEE'S DOUBLE DIP

```
                                          CH. RINKY DINK'S SIR LANCELOT
                            CH. KAPLAR'S BLACK KNIGHT
                                          CH. KAPLAR'S KUSTOM-KUT
             CH. CIN-DEE'S KNIGHT LIGHTS
                                          PLANTATION'S PILOT
                            CIN-DEE'S INTANDESCENT
                                          PLANTATION'S PARASOL
CH. CIN-DEE'S DOUBLE DIP
                                          CH. RINKY DINK'S SIR LANCELOT
                            CH. KAPLAR'S BLACK KNIGHT
                                          CH. KAPLAR'S KUSTOM-KUT
             CH. SOUTH PAWS' MY LITTLE MARGIE
                                          CH. KAPLAR'S KASSANOVA
                            SOUTH PAWS' SILVER STARLET
                                          CH. HO-WIN'S FLASHY VELVET
```

Ch. Cin-Dee's Double Dip, "Edie" was the ASC 1/89 National Best in Futurity Winner and RWB. She and her 5 champion littermates finished with national attention. She is a result of linebreeding on Ch. Kaplar's Black Knight (sire of 18 champions with limited use). She is littermate of Laura Henson's top producer, Kon Man. The extended pedigree reveals several crosses to Ch. Rinky Dink's Sir Lancelot and Ch. Lurola's Royal Lancer - top producing black and tans in breed history. Edie's sire and dam were both top producing black and tans in 1993. Ch. Cin-Dee's Knight Lights is the sire of nearly 30 champions to date including National Futurity winners. Edie, herself, is now the dam of 6 champions.

Cindy Lane
104 Highland Dr
Duncan, South Carolina 29334

Cin-Dee's Cockers
(803) 433-1464

CH. MADEZ SATURDAY NITE SPECIAL

```
                              CH. HARLANHAVEN'S HIGH AND MIGHTY
                    CH. HARLANHAVEN'S HIGH SPIRIT
                              BUTCH'S YOUNG AT HEART
          CH. KRISMYTH NEVER ON SUNDAY
                              CH. SHAM-O-JET'S BUCKY BEAVER
                    CH. KRISMYTH RESTLESS SPIRIT
                              CH. ALORAH'S GARDENIA
CH. MADEZ SATURDAY NITE SPECIAL
                              CH. SHAM-O-JET'S BUCKY BEAVER
                    CH. KRISMYTH ON TARGET
                              CH. ALORAH'S GARDENIA
          MADDIE'S KRISMYTH BONUS
                              CH. HARLANHAVEN'S HIGH SPIRIT
                    KRISMYTH BURNT TOAST
                              KRISMYTH CINNAMON TOAST
```

Katie has proven her beauty in the show ring and shared her free and merry temperament everywhere she goes. At the January 1994 American Spaniel Club show, she was awarded Best of Opposite Sex to Best of Black Variety. Loved, owned and presented by breeder Maddie Brown, she exemplifies the type and temperament of Madez Cockers.

Maddie Brown   Madez Cockers
2011 Ruby   (712) 255-8110
Sioux City, Iowa 51103

CH. JAY-CEE'S BUNCH OF BULL

```
                                        CH. DUR-BET'S PICK THE TIGER
                              CH. WINDY HILL'S TIS DEMI'S DEMON
                                        CH. WINDY HILL'S TIS DEMITASSE
                  CH. MUST-DO'S MATADOR
                                        CH. SHOESTRING SHOOTIN MATCH
                              MUST-DO MAGIC MOMENT
                                        CH. KAPLAR'S KAP-T-VATOR
      CH. JAY-CEE'S BUNCH OF BULL
                                        CH. LIZ-BAR MUSIC BOX
                              CH. FORJAY'S RUN FOR THE ROSES
                                        CH. LIZ-BAR WINTER ROSE
                  AM/BRZ CH. JAY-CEE'S JUST CHER'N IT ALL
                                        CH. JAZZMAN CLAP HANDS
                              CH. ESPECIAL'S ECSTATIC ECHO
                                        CRESTWICKE'S ESPECIAL-E CUTE
```

"B.S." is a black & tan dog with SOUNDNESS - SUBSTANCE - STYLE - BREED TYPE! This dog has it all... a good producer, lovely head, strong body, smooth neck and shoulders, long neck, hard back, good scissors bite and abundant correct coat. Combined with attitude and good temperament, he represents what Jay-Cee's stands for:

"A SYMBOL OF LOVE" for the American Cocker Spaniel.

Connie & Jim Walsh
26 East Grove St
Lombard, Illinois 60148-2322

Jay-Cee's Cockers
(708) 620-5314

CH. WESTON'S TOUCH 'O TAN

```
                                    CH. PALM HILL CARO-BU'S SOLID GOLD
                         CH. HU-MAR'S GO FOR THE GOLD
                                    CH. PALM HILL HU-MAR'S WILDFIRE
               CH. CRIG-MAR'S CON ARTIST
                                    AM/ CAN CH. MERRYHAVEN MAGNUM P.I.
                         CH. CRIG MAR SHADY LADY
                                    CH. CRIG MAR'S CAPRICE
CH. WESTON'S TOUCH O' TAN
                                    CH. PALM HILL CARO-BU'S SOLID GOLD
                         CH. GLENMURRY'S SOLID BLACK
                                    CH. GLENMURRY'S HIGHLAND CAPER
               WESTON ' N HU-MAR'S GINGER SNAP
                                    CH. KAPLAR'S KON MAN
                         CH. HU-MAR'S WITCHES BREW
                                    CH. PALM HILL HU-MAR'S BEWITCHED
```

Tanner - a beautiful dog with a beautiful pedigree. This Best of Variety Winner finished quickly with majors from the puppy class and is now starting his specials and obedience career. He is linebred on the best of Hu-Mar breeding in buff and black and every dog in his 3 generation pedigree is a producer of multiple champions. He will be dominant for beautiful heads, pretty necks and shoulders, sound rears, correct movement with a topline, and great dispositions. Tanner represents our future!

Leslie and Paul Weston
715 Lillards Ferry Rd
Versailles, Kentucky 40383

Weston Cockers and Cedar Ridge Appaloosas
(606) 873-6595
Puppies and foals occasionally

CH. GLEN ARDEN'S REAL McCOY

```
                              CH. CHESS KING'S BOARD BOSS
                   CH. FRANDEE'S FEDERAL AGENT
                              CH. FRANDEE'S PRIM N' PROPER
          CH. FRANDEE'S FORGERY
                              CH. FEINLYNE FOREMOST
                   CH. FEINLYNE FETCH AND GO
                              FEINLYNE B.T.
CH. GLEN ARDEN'S REAL MCCOY
                              CH. WINDY HILL'S 'TIS DEMI'S DEMON
                   CH. MEMOIR'S MARC IN THE DARK
                              MEMOIR'S MORNING GLORY
          GLEN ARDEN'S MOLLY MCGEE
                              MEMOIR'S STREAKER
                   CH. GLEN ARDEN'S GINGER SNAPP
                              CH. GLEN ARDEN'S PAPOOSE O'POWWOW
```

"MAC" is a multiple Best in Show and Best in Show Specialty (8 in '86) winner. He was top breed dog in '86. Sire of 55 champions. Most have his qualities: excellent temperament, overall balance, good front and sound rear, no slips, long neck with good shoulders, topline, pretty head and nice coat. At 11 years, he is in excellent condition and is the top producing living black dog. SLT/PRA clear. OFA CS 1018G30M. We ship from Ontario, Ca. Stud Fee $400.00.

Tom & Dottie McCoy
922 West 5th St
San Dimas, California 91773

Glen Arden
(818) 966-9262
(909) 599-8851

CH. SHER-RON'S QUARTERMASTER

CH. DUR BETS TARTAN
CH. PRIME TIME SUPERFLY
DOLLY'S SUGAR N' SPICE
CH. SHERRON'S MARKSMAN
CH. FORJAY'S WINTERWOOD
CH. SHERRON'S WIND SONG
CH. TALLYLYN MY LIZA LOVE
CH. SHERRON'S QUARTERMASTER
CH. LUROLA'S ROYAL LANCER
CH. SHELBYSHIRE SQUIRE C.D.
CH. DOLLY'S CERTAINLY SOMETHING
SHERRON'S GARLIC BREAD
CH. ARDEE'S TRADEMARK
SHERRON'S GIFT O'LOVE
EPPLER'S MY BRIGETTE

"Marty" finished his championship easily with three majors under all-breed and specialty judges alike. He typifies the "up on leg," hard-back, pretty heads, "un-ending showmanship," and first class temperaments that are synonymous with Sher-Rons. Sire of champions, Marty is OFA Good and permanently listed as SLT, clear for cataracts and PRA in the ASC Health Registry.

Sher-Ron's Cockers, Breeders of Top Quality Blacks, ASCOBS, and English Cocker Spaniels.

Jack & Carolanne Garlick
5001 Brownlow Rd
Knoxville, Tennessee 37938

Sher-Ron's Cockers
(615) 922-3738

CH. MISTIWIND'S HONEY BEAR

```
                              CH. PALM HILL'S KRUGERAND
                    CH. PIPER HILL'S MICHAELANGELO
                              CH. BOBWIN'S SPECIAL BLEND
          CH. ROBILL'S DESIGNER GENES
                              CH. TEMPARK'S ROCKY MT. HALE
                    CH. ROBILL'S ROCK'S ANN OF TOMPARK
                              CH. BOBWIN'S ANTICIPATION
CH. MISTIWIND'S HONEY BEAR
                              CH. MICA'S BOBWIN MODERATOR
                    CH. T-ROSE BOBWIN CORDIAL
                              CH. BOBWIN'S FASMAR FASCINATOR
          MISTWIND'S MANDATE
                              AM CAN CH. KARLYLE'S ON THE CUFF
                    MISTIWINDS CANADIAN CAPER
                              MISTIWIND'S LITTLE BIT O'LOVE
```

Ch. Mistiwind's Honey Bear was whelped April 30, 1991. Her great enthusiasm for the show ring was greatly enhanced by her best friend - Gretchen Stone of Windrush Cockers in Las Vegas. Now she's at home and her same joy of life and all it has to offer, will be passed to future children.

Janet Little
187 Winston Dr
Santa Rosa, California 95407

Mistiwind Cocker Spaniels
(707) 544-1009

CH. SIRIUS' BRASS LASS
Sept . 1987-Nov. 1991

		CH. STONEHEDGE PROOF O' THE PUDDIN'
	CH. WINDY HILL'S ROYAL PUDDIN'	
		CH. WINDY HILL'S 'TIS A WENCH
	CH. LIPTON'S CRUISIN' FOR A BRUISIN'	
		CH. HAR-DEE'S BLACK BENJI
	PATLYN NOVEMBER MAHOGANY KISS	
		CH. THURLYN ACRE TANZANIA
CH. SIRIUS' BRASS LASS		
		CH. MILRU'S KISMET TOO
	CH. MILRU'S ARABIAN KNIGHT	
		CH. MILRU'S TANDORABLE
	TABAKA'S TSETSE FLY	
		CH. DUR-BET'S TARTAN
	CH. TABAKA'S TIDBIT O'TERMITE	
		CH. TABAKA'S TIDBIT O'WYNDEN, CDX

While trying to decide which of my dogs would best represent the Kalasic Cockers, it became obvious that I should pay tribute to the lovely lady who started it all. Tessa was not my first show Cocker, but was my first champion in the breed and was to have been the foundation for my breeding program. Unfortunately, she was taken from me before this could be. Tessa is the ideal for which I continue to strive. Her style, her elegance, and intelligence are already evident in my newest puppies out of her grandniece. Even though Tessa was not in actuality the foundation for my kennel, she remains the motivating spirit behind Kalasic Cockers.

Julie Kallbacka
3703 South Hancock Rd
Magna, Utah 84044

Kalasic Kennels
(801) 250-9538

CH. M-BAR-S' TRIONIC MAN

CH. HOMESTEAD'S TRAILBLAZER
CH. HOMESTEAD'S HUCKLEBERRY
CH. HOMESTEAD'S FARMER'S DAUGHTER
CH. J-DON'S GO FOR BROKE
CH. HOMESTEAD'S WINDJAMMER
CH. HOMESTEAD'S BUTTER BRICKLE
HOMESTEAD'S COUNTRY GIRL
CH. M-BAR-S' TRIONIC MAN
CH. FEINLYNE BY GEORGE
CH. M-BAR-S' LINUS B
CH. M-BAR-S' KATY BAR THE DOOR
CH. PAT-MAR'S ADASTAR ELEGANCE
CH. LAURIM'S TRI PERFORMANCE
CH. HOMESTEAD'S SHINDIG
CH. HOMESTEAD'S COTTON GINNY

A prepotent sire - sire of eight champions in a year's time. Finished from puppy class, he was the Parti futurity stakes winner at the American Spaniel Club in New York in 1991 and went on to Best of Opposite Sex and to Best in Futurity. He is the 46th champion to carry the M-Bar-S name out of a total that currently stands at sixty-five homebred champions to date.

In Memoriam:
Muriel Barber

M-Bar-S Cockers
(917) 430-1730
Rt 5, Box 86
Roanoke, Texas 76262

CH. BIZZMAR SHORT CIRCUIT

		CH. FRANDEE'S DECLARATION
	CH. FRANDEE'S BILL O RIGHTS	
		CH. FRANDEE'S SUSAN
	CH. KAMPS' KREDIT KARD	
		CH. REXPOINTE KOJAK
	CH. KAMPS' KOUNTRY KISS	
		CH. MIRWIN'S MERRY MISS
CH. BIZZMAR SHORT CIRCUIT		
		CH. ORIENT'S PRIDE & PLEASURE
	CH. BIZZMAR BUCCANEER	
		BIZZMAR BLUESETTE
	CH. BIZZMAR BIANCA	
		CH. AL-MAR'S RUFF 'N REDDY
	CH. BIZZMAR BETHANY	
		BIZZMAR BUSY BEE

Bizzmar PRODUCING........SHOWING.......AND LOVING QUALITY COCKERS SINCE 1954. A quality dog, "Simon" is producing quality like himself. VERY SOUND in both temperament and conformation. Produces Champion Quality Red and White, Black and White, Tri, Black and ASCOB. Whelped 1/15/83, he is SLT/PRA clear...OFA CS1238G. Permanently listed in the American Spaniel Club Health Registry.

Bred, owned, and handled by :
Mary F. Galton   Bizzmar Cockers
4212 Necker Ave
Baltimore, Maryland 21236

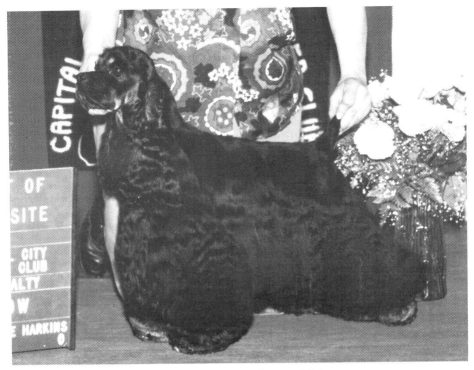

CH. BIZZMAR BOUDICCA

```
                              CH. FRANDEE'S BILL OF RIGHTS
                    CH. KAMPS' KREDIT KARD
                              CH. KAMPS' KOUNTRY KISS
          CH. BIZZMAR SHORT CIRCUIT
                              CH. BIZZMAR BUCCANEER
                    CH. BIZZMAR BIANCA
                              CH. BIZZMAR BETHANY
CH. BIZZMAR BOUDICCA
                              CH. HAYDAY HENCHMAN
                    CH. JEMAR'S MAJOR GREGG
                              JEMAR'S CRICKET
          CH. BIZZMAR GREEN-OAK'S GYPSY
                              CH. BIZZMAR BUCCANEER
                    CH. GREEN-OAK'S EBB TIDE
                              GREEN-OAK'S MORNING MIST
```

Bizzmar PRODUCING....... SHOWING....... AND LOVING QUALITY COCKERS SINCE 1954. A joy from the moment she was whelped, "Boots" is everything desirable in a show Cocker.... beauty, proper construction and movement, excellent temperament, and showmanship. As a companion, she is sweet, loving, intelligent, and friendly. SLT/PRA clear. OFA: CS-3298G. Listed in the American Spaniel Club Health Registry.

Bred, owned and handled by :
Mary F. Galton   Bizzmar Cockers
4212 Necker Ave
Baltimore, Maryland 21236

CH. GREEN-OAKS JERHICO OF JEMAR

CH . HEYDAY HEADHUNTER
CH. HEYDAY HENCHMAN
CH. SHARDELOES SELENA
CH. JEMAR'S MAJOR GREGG
CH. HEYDAY HERALD
JEMAR'S CRICKET
CH. PARKSWAY KISS ME KATE
CH. GREEN-OAKS JERHICO OF JEMAR
CH. ORIENT'S PRIDE 'N PLEASURE
CH. BIZZMAR BUCCANEER
BIZZMAR BLUESETTE
CH. GREEN-OAK'S EBB TIDE
CH. DAWN'S TRIBUTE TO HENRY
GREEN OAK'S MORNING MIST
ANELANAIA'S NUTS BUT NICE

"Jerry's" beautiful head, correct coat texture, proper movement, balance, soundness, and temperament is what made him the Best of Variety Winner at the Westminster Show in 1987. His awards include Best in Specialty Show wins, numerous Group Placements and 95 Best of Varieties. He sires champion quality black, black & tan, and buff. SLT/PRA clear, OFA: CS 1843G. He is permanently listed in the American Spaniel Club Health Registry.

Owned by: Handled by: Mary F. Galton
Mary Stacey   Bizzmar Cockers
Jemar Cockers   Breeder: Eileen Chenevert
794 Biggs Hwy   Green-Oaks Cockers
Rising Sun, Maryland 21911

PRINCESS MARGARET X, CDX, CGC

"Princess" did not have an outstanding pedigree, but she earned her CDX in Florida and Alabama. She starred in a production of "Annie" as Annie's faithful companion, "Sandy," at Jasmine Hill in Montgomery, Alabama. She also garnered one leg on her Utility Title. She spent most of her life going to schools, nursing homes, public libraries, and parades. She had two daughters with CD's, a granddaughter with a CD (High in Trial in Panama City, Florida) and a sister with a CD. She also had two children with K-9 Good Citizen Awards. When the photo above was taken, she was nine years old and in good health. She passed on at over fifteen years of age and we will surely miss her.

Margaret McRae
3837 Flowers Chapel Rd
Dothan, Alabama 36301

Rainbow Kennels
(334) 793-3264
(334) 794-2290

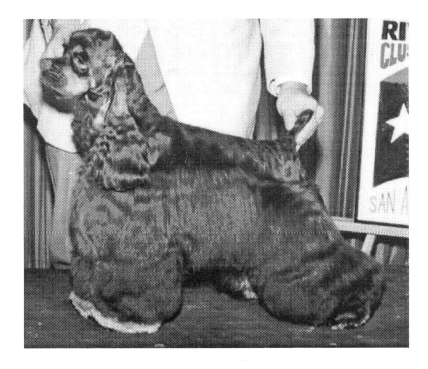

CH. JPK'S SIMPLY JAZZIE

```
                              CH. LUROLA'S EDWARD P
                  CH. LUROLA'S CLIFTON
                              CH. LUROLA'S CAROL B
         CH. TELL-TAIL'S CHASIN' SANBORN
                              CH. SANDOR'S DUTCH CHOCOLATE, CDX
                  CH. TELL-TAIL'S FUDGE FEATHERS
                              REGALIA'S FIRE N' FEATHERS
CH. JPK'S SIMPLY JAZZIE
                              CH. SHER-RON'S XTRA-ORDINARIE
                  CH. CAVALIER XTRA-SPECIAL BEAR
                              TOUCHE'S CONNIE B. HERSEY
         JPK'S TWIX R FOR KIDS
                              CH. HU-MAR'S GO FOR THE GOLD, CD
                  LORLI NATALIE WOOD
                              CH. LORLI ROSEWOOD
```

Jazz is a true example of a lovely Brown/Tan Cocker Spaniel. This bitch is sired by Ch. Tell-Tail's Chasin Sandborn. The dam is black, Ch. JPK's Twix R for Kids. Jazz is a multiple Sweeps winner who own the hearts of many.

Debbie Bertrand
Rt. 1 Box 405
Fresno, Texas 77545

JPK Cockers
(713) 980-9404 * (713) 431-1502
Handled by Jeff Wright

CH. JPK'S WINGS OF FALCON

```
                                    CH. HOMESTEAD'S WIND JAMMER
                          CH. HOMESTEAD'S SHILOH OF J-DON
                                    HOMESTEAD'S JOLENE
                  CH. THAT'S IT MILLENNIUM FALCON
                                    CH. SILVER MAPLE HERE COMES TODDY
                          CH. HI HOPES BONNIE BECKI
                                    CH. RED COLLAR'S SWEET CHARRA
CH. JPK'S WINGS OF FALCON
                                    CH. HOMESTEAD'S HAPPY CAMPER
                          CII. FAR-ACE PRETTY BOY FLOYD
                                    SPINDLER'S N J-DON'S PRESTIGE
                  CH. JPK'S BONNIE PARKER
                                    CH. MY-IDA-HO DIAMOND JIM
                          FAR-ACE N JPK DANCIN' TIL DAWN
                                    J-DON'S FAR-ACE MAD MONEY
```

This lovely parti Bitch is a combination of two outstanding pedigrees. The sire, Ch. That's It Millennium Falcon, was an ASC Best of Variety winner and producer of an ASC Variety winner. The dam, Ch. JPK's Bonnie Parker, is the daughter of one the two top producing parti colors, Ch. Far-Ace JPK Pretty Boy Floyd. Wings of Falcon has won many Best of Variety and group placements.

Debbie Bertrand and John Zolezzi
Rt. 1 Box 405
Fresno, Texas 77545

Eighty-Eights
(713) 980-9404 * (713) 431-1502
(619) 436-1256

CH. SHER-RON'S EVENING ATTIRE, CD, TDI, CGC

CH. FORJAY'S WINTERWOOD
CH. COTTONWOOD'S CONGRESSMAN
LORLI GIGI
BISS CH. PALM HILL CARO-BU'S SOLID GOLD
CH. KAMP'S SILVERSMITH
CH. PALM HILL'S TIGER LILY, CD
CH. HU-MAR'S HANKY PANKY CD
CH. SHER-RON'S EVENING ATTIRE, CD, TDI, CGC
CH. DUR-BET'S TARTAN
CH. PRIME TIME SUPERFLY
DOLLY'S SUGAR N' SPICE
SHER-RON'S MADE TO ORDER
CH. FORJAY'S WINTERWOOD
CH. SHER-RON'S WIND SONG
CH. TALLYLYNN MY LIZA LOVE

Chantrel Cockers is proud to present Velvet, our foundation bitch. Velvet finished her championship easily with three specialty majors and two all breed Best of Varities and proved that she has brains in her pretty head by passing the Canine Good Citizenship Test and earning a Companion Dog obedience title. Our breeding program is continuing into the next generation with her handsome black son, Ch. Chantrel's Cinnamon Twist. Velvet is enjoying retirement and rules the house, earning the title "Queen of the Known Universe." But, Velvet is a benevolent monarch and believes that all of her subjects should be permitted to adore her. So, please form a line to the right and wait your turn to pet her- no pushing or shoving; ooo-ing and ahh-ing is permitted! Portrait by Carol Goozey

Evelyn P. Bravo   Chantrel Cocker Spaniels
715 Redway Lane   (713) 480-1083
Houston, Texas 77062-4218

BIS, BISS CH. DALIN'S WAY COOL

```
                                CH. HOMESTEAD'S HUCKLEBERRY
                   CH. J-DON'S GO FOR BROKE
                                CH. HOMESTEAD'S BUTTER PICKLE
          CH. DUNMORR'S POCKET ROCKET
                                AM/CAN CH. MOODY'S MAGIC TRI
                   CH. MOODY'S COURTROOM MAGIC
                                CH. BARB'S FOXY LADY
BIS, BISS CH. DALIN'S WAY COOL
                                CH. DUNMORR'S KALVIN KLINE
                   CH. B-SKY'S WRANGLER COWBOY
                                CHE-LEE'S SKY CRICKETTE
          CH.  CHARSI'S CLASSICAL FANTASY
                                AM/CAN CH. KAMP'S KHARGE KARD
                   CH. GAMMON'S GLAD TIDINGS
                                CH. GAMMON'S GEISHA GIRL
```

The Parti Tri-Color dog pictured, Ch. Dalin's Way Cool, was the top winning Cocker Spaniel all varieties in the Northeast in 1994. He won three Best in Shows, twenty Sporting Group I's, thirteen Cocker Spaniel Specialty Best of Breeds, all in a very short specials career of only ten months. In his first year at stud, ten of his puppies finished their championships, many with Specialty Sweepstakes and Sporting Group wins. We are proud of "Dude" and what he -- and we -- have accomplished in both the breed competition ring and as a top producer of quality Cocker Spaniels.

Linda Donaldson
78 Pinehill Road
Tolland, Connecticut 06084

Dalin
(203) 875-6865

CH. REGAL'S SOCK IT TO 'EM, CGC

```
                                    CH. WINDY HILL'S TIS DEMI'S DEMON
                    CH. MUST-DO'S MATADOR
                                    MUST-DO'S MAGIC MOMENT
            CH. REGAL'S SOCK HOP
                                    CH. SPANKY'S GANG III
                    CH. HARRAN'S THE CLASSIC ONE
                                    CH. HARRAN'S SILVER MIST
CH. REGAL'S SOCK IT TO 'EM, CGC
                                    CH. WINDY HILL'S TIS DEMI'S DEMON
                    CH. MUST DO'S MATADOR
                                    MUST DO'S MAGIC MOMENT
            CH. REGAL'S JUST CLOWIN'
                                    CH. RINKY DINK'S SIR LANCELOT
                    CH. REGAL'S SEND IN THE CLOWN
                                    CH. HARRAN'S APRIL MISTY MORNIN'
```

Matt, a true sporting Cocker, has outstanding movement, structure and coat. Matt finished his championship very quickly taking 5 points, including one major, at his first show - the Houston Astrohall in 1992. Matt has an overwhelming willingness to please which he expresses in his work with mentally ill individuals as a Delta Society Therapy dog. In his free time, Matt loves to show off in agility. Matt is from a top producing bloodline, SLT/PRA clear, OFA certified, and much loved by all who meet him. Matt will surely provide a strong foundation - for he possesses all of the qualities we strive for here at Windswept!

Jerry & Laurie Ables
6 Rippled Pond Place
The Woodlands, Texas 77382

Windswept
(409) 321-6096

AM/CAN CH. WHEATLAND'S WALKABOUT TRAVELER

CH. J-DON'S GO FOR BROKE
CH. SHARADE J-DON'S PARTI ANIMAL
D-DANDEE'S SHOSHANNA SHANDEE
CH. KEEPSAKE NEW KID ON THE BLOCK
CH. HOMESTEAD'S EAZE CASSIDY KID
J-DON'S SKYE IS THE LIMIT
J-DON'S EAZE CALAMITY JANE
AM/CAN CH. WHEATLAND'S WALKABOUT TRAVELER
CH. MARQUIS IT'S THE ONE
CH. STANWOOD BOURNE IDENITY
CH. MARQUIS FLASH DANCER
TOKAY'S FOREVER AMBER
CH. CAROLINE'S SNOW FLIGHT
CHARBARI SWISS DOTTED
CHARBARI SIMPLY SMASHING

"Ernie" has a lovely out-going "happy camper" attitude which he is passing along to his off-spring. He is producing open well marked pups -- predominently girls. At the Jan., 1994 ASC Nationals, he went 4th in a class of 27; at the specialty on Sunday he went WD over 44 others for a five point major. He finished in Canada in five shows with four extra points. He has lovely movement with his tail up and wagging. At "Justmy" we breed for movement and attitude.

Betty Willroth   Justmy Cockers
1679 Athens Ave   (209) 323-1311
Clovis, California 93611-7379

CH. AVALON'S DRAGON SLAYER

```
                                      CH. DAL-MAR'S BILLY JACK
                           CH. DAL MAR N TOUCHE'S MAKE MY DAY
                                      CH. DAL-MAR'S DON'T EAT THE DAISIES
            CH. AVALON'S NO MISTAKE
                                      CH. MARQUIS MAGNUM
                           CH. AVALON'S BRAVO BLACK CAT
                                      CH. MARQUIS SWEET DIANE
CH. AVALON'S DRAGON SLAYER
                                      CH. DAL-MAR'S BILLY JACK
                           CH. DAL-MAR N TOUCHE'S MAKE MY DAY
                                      CH. DAL-MAR'S DON'T EAT THE DAISIES
            AVALON'S ANGEL BY DAY
                                      CH. DANZATA'S MR. ED
                           AVALON'S ASPEN
                                      AVALON'S IT'S A BIT TOO MUCH
```

"Dragon" is continuing the Avalon tradition of finishing with multiple Best of Variety wins. Gorgeous fronts, correct upper forearm and strong driving rears are a must. Lovely pet puppies in all colors, including chocolates and sables. We have bred or owned 128 champions (Labradors and Cockers) since 1965. All breeding stock have current eye exams and hip X-rays.

Jean Nelson
620 W. Co Rd 16
Loveland, Colorado 80537

Avalon Kennels
(970) 663-6955
FAX (970) 593-9462

CH. EMPIRE'S BROOKLYN DODGER

CH. DAL-MAR'S DOUBLE DEALER
CH. DAL-MAR'S BILLY JACK
BANCU FAITH & BEGORRAH
CH. TERJE'S THUNDERBOLT
CH. SHA-DON'S SUGARBEAR OF SWANK'S, CD
CH. SWANK'S SHORT N' SWEET
SWANK'S SEPTEMBER SONG
CH. EMPIRE'S BROOKLYN DODGER
CH. DAL-MAR'S DOUBLE DEALER
CH. DAL-MAR'S BILLY JACK
BANCU FAITH & BEGORRAH
HARLANHAVEN'S HEAVENLY BLISS
CH. HARLANHAVEN'S HIGH AND MIGHTY
TERJE'S SWEETEST TABU
CH. SWANK'S SHORT 'N SWEET

"Dodger" started off his show career by winning the futurity at American Spaniel Club's 1990 summer show. Defeating the most dogs from puppy class won him American Cocker Magazine's 1990 puppy of the year. Dodger is the only dog to win a futurity and to have sired two American Spaniel Club Futurity winners. He has produced over 20 champions to date, including ASC winners, Specialty winners, and All Breed Best In Show winners. Dodger defeated more Cockers in 1993 and won 17 Specialties in one year. His record to date is 11 All Breed BIS, 29 Specialty BIS (this is the all time record), 48 Group 1sts, and 56 other placements.

Jeff L. Wright
4827 SE Hwy 40
Topeka, Kansas 66607

Terje Cockers
(913) 379-5541

CH. SNOWCLOUD'S HAPPY STARBRITE

```
                              CH. REXPOINTE FLYING DUTCHMAN
                 CH. SIGNATURE SOLITAIRE
                              CH. REGALIA'S TELL TAIL TWIRL
            CH. DAL-MAR'S SNOWCLOUD BEAR
                              CH. REPERTOIRE RENEGADE
                 MO MASTERS FIRST LADY
                              HI POINT SMOOTH AS SILK
CH. SNOWCLOUD'S HAPPY STARBRITE
                              CH. MARGON'S LIL CEASAR
                 SWANK'S HAPPY SNOWCLOUD, CDX
                              AR-BEE'S SWEET SHELLY
            SNOWCLOUD'S SUGAR AND SPICE
                              CH. SHA-DON'S SUGARBEAR OF SWANK'S, CD
                 KATY DID'S PEACHES & CREAM
                              SWANKS SEPTEMBER SONG
```

Looking for a Best Friend? Then you'll want to consider a beautiful Snowcloud Cocker! Bred to love and be loved, this line of Cockers is known to excel in intelligence, beauty, health, and good temperament. The quality is exemplified by the coveted Dog World Award earned by Snowcloud's "Zip," as well as the many Obedience Titles awarded to other Snowcloud Cockers. But it doesn't stop there. Many Championship titles have been earned by this line in the Breed Ring, supported by numerous "Best of Variety's" and Sporting Group placements. If you live in a home where love abounds, but something is missing, one of these lovable dogs could be your best friend. "Star" is shown exclusively by Jackie Downing, Jac-E-Dee.

Alice Horton
RR 3, Fairfield, Illinois 62837
(618) 842-3056

SNOWCLOUD

CH. SHALIMAR'S IN COMMAND

CH. DAL-MAR'S DOUBLE DEALER
CH. DAL-MAR'S BILLY JACK
BANCU FAITH & BEGORRAH
CH. TERJE'S THUNDERBOLT
CH. SHADON SUGAR BEAR OF SWANK
CH. SWANK'S SHORT N' SWEET
SWANK'S SEPTEMBER SONG
CH. SHALIMAR'S IN COMMAND
CH. CAMPBELL'S COLOR ME CANDYMAN
CH. ANDMOR'S DOUBLE DISTINCTIVE
ANDMOR'S DOUBLE DELIGHT
CH. SHALIMAR'S SOFT TOUCH
CH. SANDY HILL'S SOLAR OF MY LISLEE
CH. SHALIMAR'S DEVASTATION, CD
CH. SHALIMAR'S OLYMPIAD, CD

They say a picture is worth a thousand words, and this is it.
Ch. Shalimar's In Command
Command: to give an order; to direct; to have authority over; to have control.
#1 Cocker Spaniel (All varieties), 1989 and
#1 Parti -Color Cocker Spaniel, 1990
In limited use Larry has sired 25+ champions with more on the way.

*Webster's definition.

Breeder: MaryAnn Meekins
712 John Anderson Hwy
Flagler Beach, FL 32136

Shalimar Kennels
(904) 439-3950

CH. SOUTHERN COMFORT'S SWEET SAVANNAH

CH. WARD'S WINTERSET
CH. GING'S ALYDAR
CH. GING'S PHOEBE FIREWORKS
CH. GLENMURRAY'S DECLARATION
CH. JUBAN'S GEORGIA JAZZ
FRANDEE'S JAZZERCISE
CH. FRANDEE'S FAR OUT
CH. SOUTHERN COMFORT'S SWEET SAVANNAH
CH. MY-IDA-HO DIAMOND JIM
AM/PHIL CH. MY-IDA-HO DIAMONDS TO GO

MY-IDA-HO PRIDE N' JOY
AM/CAN CH. SPRINGHILL'S SWEET N SASSY
CH. MY-IDA-HO DIAMOND JIM
CAN CH. SPRINGHILL'S ASH TREE MEADOW
DESERENE'S TRI DREAMING

If there is such a thing as a perfect friend, it could definitely be a Cocker. It is a pleasure to share life with such a beautiful creature who can be your comfort and protection, make you smile when you are blue, share your bed (and sometimes your dinner), and still make you burst with pride in the ring. Our foundation bitch, Sarah, (Am/Can Springhill's Sweet N' Sassy) embodies the qualities I value most in a Cocker and passes them on to her offspring. Sarah gave us our first two homebred champions, Southern Comfort's Rodeo Romeo and Southern Comfort's Sweet Savannah. Like their Dam, they have beautiful toplines, great angulation, easy care coats, and that special attitude. Sarah has several offspring and grandnieces and nephews pointed and close to completing their AKC titles in the near future. We will continue to breed for a sound Cocker in the future, with Sarah setting our type-A Cocker with a competitive attitude that can still be your best friend.

Jim and Glenda Thorn
1326 Mt. Pleasant Rd.
Muscle Shoals, Alabama 35661

Southern Comfort Cockers
(205) 446-9327

CH. TRIANNE'S OH HENRY!!

BIS MEX/AM CH. TAGALONG'S MACHO MAN
INT/AM CH. DERANO'S DARE DEVIL
CH. DERANO'S MOLLY BROWN
CH. FRANDEE'S FOUR ON FLOOR
CH. GING'S ALYDAR
CH. FRANDEE'S BUBBLE UP
FRANDEE'S POTPOURRI
CH. TRIANNE'S OH HENRY!!
CH. RAMBLEWOOD'S RICH N' CHIPS
CH. STA-MARS CHOC-O-LITE
CH. TRIANNON MONKEY BUSINESS
TRIANNE'S CHOCOLATE KISS
CH. BARJOHN'S MOCHA MAN
TRIANNE'S MOCHA MISS
AMOR'S CHOCOLATE SWISS MISS

Trianne Kennels have been breeding sound and sane Cockers for over 10 years. We have produced over 20 champions in numerous colors, but now only concentrate on Parti-colors, including rarer chocolate/whites (like Henry) and chocolate/tris. Health and temperament are extremely important to us. All stock is OFA certified, SLT/PRA clear and T-3/T-4 blood levels are normal. Being a small breeder, all puppies are raised in our kitchen, underfoot. All pets are sold spayed or neutered with limited registrations to responsible homes. All show puppies sold are puppies we would spend money to show, they are not seconds. We have champions and companions all over the world.

At Trianne .....our Pride is showing........

Dr. Dennis and Roxanne Harris-Parks
Rt 1 Box 1244
Waco, Texas 76712-9721

Trianne Kennels
Phone (817) 848-9147
Fax (817) 848-9361

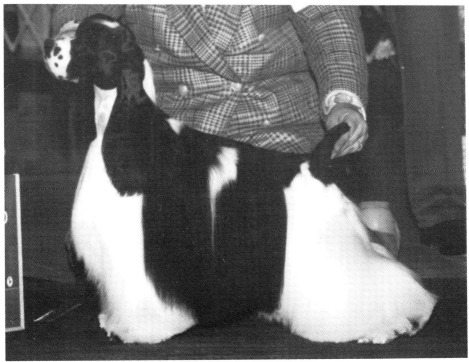

CH. DAZLIN DANGEROUS JADE

```
                                          CH. DAL MAR'S BILLY JACK
                        CH. TERJE'S THUNDERBOLT
                                          CH. SWANK'S SHORT N SWEET
            CH. SHALIMAR'S IMPERATOR
                                          CH. ANDMOR'S DOUBLE DISTINCTIVE
                        CH. SHALIMAR'S SOFT TOUCH
                                          CH. SHALIMAR'S DEVASTATION
CH. DAZLIN DANGEROUS JADE
                                          CH. LEGEND DUDLEY DORIGHT
                        CH. GLORILAND'S JEREMIAH
                                          CH. BONNY JAY'S HOSANNA
            B SKY'S MYSTIC SARA
                                          CH. SOUTHWIND SHIKARI
                        B SKY'S MYSTIC DANIELLE
                                          CHE -LEE'S SKY CRICKETTE
```

Jaws is out of our first parti-color breeding at Dazlin. He won the 9 to 12 month July, '91 ASC Summer National Futurity class and finished as Best of Winners at the January, '92 ASC Flushing Spaniel Show. "Specialed" very lightly over the Summer of 1992, Jaws won three Best of Varieties, two Specialty Bests in Show, and an Award of Merit at the July, '92 ASC Summer National. Three bitch littermates also finished with multiple majors and Best of Opposite Sex wins. We're very thankful for this great beginning.

Becki and Dale Zaborowski
6732 Romain Dr
Acworth, Georgia 30102-1151

DAZLIN

Dazlin Cockers
(404) 974-7931

months before you attempt to show. You may want to start showing at a local "match show." These are practice shows for both conformation and obedience. They offer no points toward a title, but they are usually small, with limited competition and no pressure and they are a good place to begin to learn the dog show game.

Conformation and obedience are two very different kinds of activities and they frequently attract different kinds of personalities in both dogs and people. Even the dress is different. People who show obedience dogs wear casual clothes. Many obedience people feel that dark pants help blend with the dog and mask mistakes. Shirts and pants, even for women is the normal attire. In conformation, especially in the East, women almost always wear dresses, suits with skirts, or skirts and blouses. Men wear sports coats and ties, except on very hot days when the judge may indicate that the coat may be disregarded. Men are seldom seen without a tie, jeans are not appropriate, and women are almost never seen in pants. In California, and some other areas, golf shirts and pants are sometimes worn, though jeans and T-shirts are never considered appropriate.

The American Cocker Spaniel is also good in Agility. Begun in 1977 in England, Agility is an obstacle course for dogs. It is fun, fast and growing in popularity each year. Dogs go through a series of obstacles, over a bridge, over teeter totters, through tunnels and barrels, between poles, and over A-frames. Brought to the United States in 1985, Agility has already spread from coast to coast, has a Final Competition at the Astrodome each year, and has spawned two national clubs and hundreds of local clubs. Dogs must be over 6 months old, and able to compete through obstacles off lead. Dogs compete against time over the obstacles and lose points for failing to complete an obstacle as described. Qualifying scores add toward titles, but high score dogs at an event are also recognized. Call your local kennel club for details of Agility Clubs in your area; most kennel clubs have at least a few members who are active in agility and new clubs are forming every year.

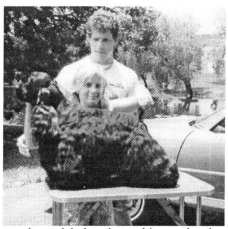

The American Cocker is still used in the field. Although it is impossible to use a dog in full conformation show coat, many Cockers in a working clip will be happy to pursue the sport for which they were bred. Recently, a bitch, finished as a conformation champion, became the first AKC Master Hunter titled American cocker Spaniel in history. Her owner started her with birds as a young dog (see chapter on Training) and she is said to have won the title easily. If you are interested in a Cocker for field work, be prepared to work with your dog from an early age just as you would with any field breed and don't be discour-

Dog shows include classes for Jr. exhibitors, such as this young lady who is practicing with her Cocker. During examination by the judge, Cockers are placed on a table such as this one.

aged by members of the hunting community who tend to dismiss the Cocker as no longer being suitable for the work.

Recently, the AKC has added the Canine Good Citizen test. They are recognizing the need for responsible dog ownership, and the recognition of well trained pets. Most clubs put on a CGC test at least once a year. This test, which lasts most of a day, tests the dog's ability to do basic obedience and his attitude in meeting new people and new situations. If he passes the test, he is awarded a CGC title. These tests are growing in popularity and more and more dogs are showing up with CGC attached to their names.

Temperament Testing is somewhat similar, though it is not done through AKC. These tests require a dog to meet friendly strangers, hostile strangers, neutral strangers, and a variety of situations. Again, the test will take up the better part of a day, but the title earned will stay with the dog for life.

HOW TO KNOW A STAR

Dog showing is a subjective sport. People who show talk about the fine points of conformation. But almost everyone agrees that *quality* and *balance* are just as important as any single asset. Balance is reflected both in the way the front and rear of a dog go together and in the way a dog moves. It refers to the proportions of the dog, and how they all fit together. But there is another factor in a top winning dog. It is elusive, and cannot truly be defined, but it is called *presence*. One breeder described a retired show dog at eight years of age. "He came into a large room, stood there and looked at you. Everything else in the room faded away. I have never seen a photograph that does him justice. The memory of him that day is implanted in my mind forever." A show dog with presence can sometimes have a few faults. He may not be as perfect as another dog, but he has a style, a quality that sets him apart like an actor or a model. He is charismatic, and a judge is attracted to him.

Though a different color, black and tan dogs show with black dogs in the black variety.

Some dogs are called *package dogs.* They are nice in a number of ways. They may have a good head, though not as good as some other entries'. But they are good movers, and have sound conformation, balance and presence. They have no large faults, so they go together in a well balanced package, and they are strong in a number of ways. This is what makes a truly great show dog.

But remember, there is no such thing as a perfect dog, or one which wins all the time. The top winning dog at Madison Square Garden, or at the Nationals, may fail to get a ribbon the next day under a different judge. Opinions of judges will be different depending on their personal experiences and beliefs. The stronger the competition is between good dogs, the more disagreement there is between the winners because the finer points of judging require personal evaluation. There are no numerical standards. One characteristic may be listed as a fault, but so might another on a different dog and there is nothing to say which is better or which is worse. A judge may be looking at one dog with a good neck and head but a bad tailset, while another has a wonderful topline but a common head. These are values which must be subjectively weighed by a judge. What a judge ultimately points at (selects as his winner) depends on his personal beliefs of which is a more serious fault, and what good points he values. Perhaps he will go with a dog which has no faults, but no outstanding features either. What is often taken as "crooked" judging is simply a matter of personal values on the part of the judge which may differ from those of the spectator or exhibitor. Remember, we do not ask a judge to tell us what he thinks is a perfect American Cocker Spaniel. We ask him his opinion in picking the best of what is in front of him that day! Like people, dogs may have good and bad days where they are more or less interested in showing. How well a dog LIKES to show is an important element, and gives him the "presence" he needs to be a winner.

There are no hard and fast rules that define a show dog. Any dog with an AKC number can be a show dog by paying the entry fee, and if he has no disqualifying faults, he will be allowed to compete to the extent of completing his class. Some dogs are so average that they will consistently place under almost all judges, even in strong competition, but they will never win for although they have no faults, they have no great assets either. Others will win one day under a judge who appreciates their good qualities, and lose another day under a judge who puts emphasis on an area where they are weak. These dogs have an up and down career, but will probably still finish before the dog with no faults but no great assets.

Keep this in mind when you are buying a show dog, and keep it in mind when you are beginning to show. And remember what one of our breeders said, "A good judge is one who puts up my dog, a bad judge puts up someone else's dog, and a terrible judge puts up my worst enemy's dog!" What this means is that dog showing is a competitive sport. Over the years, exhibitors learn to appreciate certain things in a dog and dislike others. Breeders develop their own style within their kennel and dogs which are not of that style are "inferior" in their minds. But they are not the judge. The judge may agree with them one day, and disagree with them another day. All of this is to say that if you buy a dog, one of the worst things you can do is take it to a show and ask all the other exhibitors what they think of it. The opinions you get back are more likely to reflect the feelings of the individual exhibitor toward the style, or even the breeder of the dog, than they are to be an absolute evaluation of the dog.

Parti-colored dogs are two or more solid, well-broken colors, one of which must be white: black and white, red and white (the red may range from lightest cream to darkest red), brown and white, and roans or sable and white, to include any such color combination with tan points. Roans are classified as parti-colors and may be any of the usual roaning patterns. The white must cover at least ten percent (10%).

If you are interested in showing, go to a show and see how your dog does in competition. If he wins, enjoy your success. If he loses several shows, consider that he may not be developed enough (if he is still young) or that you might not be able to show him to his best advantage. Find a professional handler, and ask him or her about showing your dog, or at least evaluating your dog. These people handle a number of different breeds from a wide variety of breeders. They know, overall, what a quality dog is and what it takes to get a dog finished. They are a more objective source of information than competing breeders or exhibitors.

Sometimes a judge will talk to you if you wait until after his assignment is over, though he is not required to do so and some do not like talking to exhibitors or novice owners. And sometimes a dog which cannot win as a puppy or young adult will mature into a fine show dog; he simply needs time to develop. The complexity of dog showing is one of the things that interests and fascinates people in the sport, and keeps them dedicated in time and money for many years.

Since the American Cocker Spaniel is considered a "coat" breed, care and condition of the coat is very important. It may take several years to develop a good coat on a dog, and it will take the new exhibitor many years to learn how to maximize the coat which nature has provided. For that reason, many new owners put their dog with a handler if they are interested in showing, and simply leave them there for the duration of his show life. Many a handler has become frustrated and furious over the condition of the coat after a winning show dog has had a "visit" home. It takes three to six hours of grooming a week to keep a Cocker in show coat, not counting the hours spent the day of the show. It also takes conditioning, good food, and several "tricks of the trade" to keep the coat from matting, being torn or breaking. One trip outside in bad weather, running through the bushes or playing in the mud, may do damage which will take months of care to fix!

Obedience and Agility dogs may carry any kind of a clip which is appropriate for the owner to care for. These are working dogs, and their competition is based on their ability to work, not on the condition of their coat and their conformation. Any dog with AKC papers may show in obedience, even if it has been spayed or neutered. Dogs or bitches which have been spayed or neutered may not show in conformation classes.

Most breeders will not guarantee that a puppy will be a great show dog. They will sell a pup based on pedigree and what other, older siblings have done in the ring, and what the puppy looks like. The longer a breeder has bred and shown, the better idea he or she will have or how much POTENTIAL a pup has. But there are seldom guarantees because there are so many variables. The area of the country a dog shows in will make a difference in how fast he finishes. Who handles him and how well he is conditioned and presented will make a difference. How much the dog ENJOYS showing will make a difference. And even experiences he has in the ring during his first few months of showing will make a difference.

Novice owners frequently take a young dog to a show, and when it does not win the first time or two, the begin to drag it around to other breeders and judges and inquire about its faults. This is very counterproductive, because all it does is call everyone's attention to the negative part of the dog, so that even when he does develop and would normally begin to win, everyone remembers the faults that have been pointed out early in the

dog's career. Also, remember it is easier for people to make negative comments about a potential competitor than it is to recognize the good qualities and point out how to best set off the strengths. That is like asking a competing coach how to improve another team! And, if you have not bought a pup from the local breeders, they may resent the fact that they were overlooked when you went outside the area. Even if you bought your dog from a local breeder, other breeders in the area may comment on the dog (either in a negative or positive way) with more of an eye on how much they like the person who sold you the dog than on how nice the dog really is. More than one dog has been sent back to a breeder because the

novice owner did not feel it was "show quality," and the breeder has finished it easily.

NEVER EXPECT ANYONE TO GUARANTEE THAT A PUPPY WILL BE A GROUP PLACING DOG. Group placings are dependent on so many different things, from the competition that day to the early care a dog has received. Many people who want a group placing dog simply try to buy an older dog who has already started his show career and done well. Often handlers will find a dog they think has great promise and approach an owner about purchasing it. Sometimes people who want a group placing dog will simply offer to "back" a dog which is already being shown and winning. This means that the "backer" puts his or her name on the dog's papers as owner and receives the fame for the dog's wins, and in return pays the bills to a greater or lesser extent depending on the arrangement. Several Westminster Winners have been "owned" by backers who never bred or owned another dog of that breed, and who have no kennel and no intentions of ever breeding. When the dog was finished showing, he simply went back to the original owner who used him or her for breeding purposes, and gave the dog a home for the rest of its life.

TRAVEL AND SHIPPING

*T*he first opportunity a puppy has to travel is when he goes to his new home. In some cases, you may not be able to find the kind of Cocker you are looking for locally. It is more important to find the right dog than to locate something fast or close. If you have a choice of driving eight or ten hours or flying a dog, flying is an option to think about. Although some breeders were very much against shipping by airlines, most reported that Cockers do very well during flights. Puppies generally go to sleep with the roar of the engines and arrive in good condition, bouncing out of their airline crates to meet their new families with enthusiasm.

Some breeders thought flying was easier than a long car ride since pups more often get carsick than airsick. Long car rides mean that the pup will need to stop to get water and go to the bathroom. At roadside rest stops he will be exposed to other dogs, or the leavings of other dogs. Instead of an adjustment to the airplane and the adjustment to the new home, the puppy must make the adjustment to several places where he stops along·the way, to the fact that he is traveling in a new car with new humans, and to the physical problem that there is seldom a quiet place for him to sleep in the car when he becomes tired. Twists and turns on the road may be hard on his stomach, and the temperature in the car goes up and down with every stop.

Flying a puppy is relatively easy. A puppy may not fly until it is eight weeks old. He should never be shipped before the first shot has been given and a period of several days to a week has passed in order to develop the required immunity and reduce stress. It is standard for the buyer to pay for the freight and the dog before it is shipped. A responsible breeder relies on his reputation to assure you that you will like the puppy you receive. If he began to ship puppies "on approval," some buyers would use the chance to shop for a puppy by having the pup sent in just to look at it. Puppies are not mail order merchandise, to be ordered, viewed and returned at will. Talk to the breeder enough to be sure you feel comfortable before you buy.

There are two ways to ship a dog or puppy. "Counter to Counter" is the term used to cover priority parcel. Some airlines call this method "dash," "express," or other terms created by the airline marketing department. Dogs are picked up at the oversized baggage claim area in the passenger terminal. There is a shorter layover time necessary at plane changes; only thirty minutes is required, as opposed to one to two hours required for regular freight. And the temperature limitations are less rigid, allowing a dog to fly in a hotter or colder temperature since he is hand carried. The disadvantage for some breeds is that there is a size and weight limitation on the crate size. Luckily, most Cockers will meet the size requirements even when fully grown. It is also more expensive than freight, usually costing around $95, depending on the airlines. But it is a flat fee, no matter where the destination or point of origin are in the continental United States. For that reason, it is sometimes cheaper to ship this way if, for example, the puppy is being shipped from Virginia to California. The shipping cost must be paid prior to shipping, meaning that the breeder must pay for the shipping at his end. This means that you will have to send a check to the breeder when you purchase the puppy, and the breeder will have to call ahead and find out the exact shipping cost. You will also need to make arrangements for a crate.

Cockers make good camping partners. They are hearty and hardy and love new things and new adventures.

A second method of shipping is freight. The dog is dropped off and picked up at the freight terminal. You will need two hours between flights for plane changes. The cost is usually cheaper, about $70 for the flight with the rate varying with the length of the trip. At this time you can buy a crate from the airline for $35 to $55. Using freight, you can pay for the freight and the crate collect when the dog arrives. But a dog may not be shipped if the temperature is below thirty degrees or above ninety degrees.

Although there are some stories of dogs being mishandled or dying during shipping, one breeder said she has shipped dogs over half a million air miles over the years and never had a problem. Although rumors abound, we could not find a single breeder who had directly had a problem of any consequence.

If you have picked up your pup at the airport, bring him directly home; do not use the opportunity to visit friends and show him off. He needs to see his new home, have quiet time to get adjusted, and get food and water. Most breeders will not send food or water with the pup. A full stomach can lead to airsickness, and water bowls tip as the crate is carried and leave the bedding wet and cold. Water, if left in a crate, should be in a special spill-proof container such as a rabbit bottle.

Bring the pup home, let him inspect the new area, and give him a bed, food and water immediately. With a full stomach and a little quiet, he will be himself in a short time.

For some pups, it may take a day or two to adjust to a new home. This may be true whether he is shipped or picked up by car. Always give a puppy about a week to learn how to behave without his littermates. Remember, a dog is a pack animal and the puppy must now recognize a new pack, i.e., your family members. He will need to learn new things such as the floorplan of the house, new hours and new patterns.

The next time your dog might have a chance to fly might be on vacation with you. Check the dog in as excess luggage and he will fly with you for a minimal cost. Pick him up at oversize baggage. It is not uncommon to see several dogs or cats from the same flight arriving as luggage with their owners. Some dogs actually begin to enjoy flying, getting excited and happy when they arrive at the airport.

Dogs may not travel on trains.

If you are traveling by car and stopping in hotels, all of our breeders felt it was very important to bring along a crate. Wire crates will fold flat for easy traveling, setting up in a hotel room with only a few quick moves. Breeders, who spend many weekends traveling with their dogs to shows, are especially concerned that people traveling with dogs not get a bad name. They encourage all pet owners who travel with dogs to remember that a dog in a hotel room is NOT at home. Many perfectly well trained pets will destroy or soil a hotel room as they would NEVER do at home. When a dog enters a hotel room, there are dozens of strange smells. Cockers are a retrieving breed with a good sense of smell, and they are curious. On top of that they are attached to their families. When left alone in a hotel room while the family goes out to dinner, or at night when the family is asleep, the Cocker may be busy investigating the smells, marking the new territory, tasting the drapes or carpet, and digging in the corners to see what he can find.

From the dog's point of view, the crate smells like home; it is his "den" which has thoughtfully been brought along for him, and he will appreciate the level of comfort it provides for him in a strange place. And a crate in a hotel room is definitely a better alternative for a day of family sightseeing than leaving the dog in the car.

Another use for a crate is if traveling to outdoor events during the summer. A crate taken out of the car, placed in the shade and draped with a space blanket is a good place for the dog during a baseball game or picnic where he is not invited. NEVER LEAVE A DOG IN A CAR IN THE HEAT OF SPRING AND SUMMER, OR THE EX-TREME COLD OF WINTER.

If you are traveling with a dog, be sure to bring plenty of food and water, bowls for food and water, and a leash. Even a dog that stays around the house is likely to become excited and disoriented in a strange place and a leash is good insurance, and responsible dog ownership. It will keep him from going up to people he does not know and who may not want the "visit," from wandering into traffic or from getting lost. Other helpful items to travel with are Pepto Bismol tablets in case he gets hold of something that does not agree with him, Dramamine for carsickness (especially if it is a young dog who has not ridden in a car often), Benadryl for insect bites, and flea spray, especially if you are near the beach. Having these things on hand when you need them can be especially helpful and take some of the stress out of travel. Many owners find it helpful to have a special suitcase for the dog with these items, blankets, toys, and a towel which can be used to wipe off feet in the winter or soaked in water to cool the dog in the summer.

If you are traveling by car with a puppy, take a few precautions to help make the trip easier. Do not feed him for an hour or so before you leave. Take him for a walk right before departure so that he has every opportunity to relieve himself. Take along a bed or box or crate and toys or blankets that he is used to. Something familiar to accompany him will help him feel comfortable. Don't let him travel with his head out the window; he can get grit or wind in his eyes. He does not realize how fast the car is moving and if he sees something interesting, he may try to jump out and investigate it. Stop every few hours to let him get a drink of water and exercise and relieve himself. But be sure to keep him on a leash so he does not dart out in front of a car or approach a strange dog which may not be friendly toward him.

If you are traveling and intend to leave the dog at home, there are three choices: you can kennel your dog, leave him in the care of a friend or relative, or set up some kind of care for him at your home. A kennel is the safest and easiest way to care for your dog when you are away. Cockers often do not care for strangers and many of our breeders felt they did better in a kennel, where strangers left them alone, than in the home of a friend or family member they did not know well. Other pets already in the home may also be a problem, as they may not always be excited about a house guest!

A reputable, clean kennel where the dog can have his own run is probably the best bet for anything more than a night or two stay. The barking of other dogs and the tendency for dogs to entertain themselves by running the fence line between runs may mean that your Cocker returns from an extended kennel stay with a bad habit of barking or running his fence at home; a day or two to adjust to being home and some stern, sharp words from you should correct the situation.

If you intend to leave your dog home with a petsitter, be sure your dog area is secure, has plenty of shade and shelter, and that your dog likes and will obey the temporary caretaker. Too often a dog will slip past a stranger and get lost.

If you are counting on someone coming into the house to feed and care for him be sure that they are reliable. Many areas of the country have professionals who are *petsitters*. These people come into the home, check on pets and care for them, and keep an eye on the house at the same time. Professional petsitters offer the advantage of keeping the dog at home where he feels comfortable and at the same time, there is someone in and out of the home. *The success of this method depends on the security of your yard* (or the area where the dog is housed). If there is a yard or pool man going in and out, for example, the gate may not be secured and the dog may slip out looking for his "family." If the fencing is not secure or the shelter is not adequate, this is not a good alternative.

Finally, the reliability of the petsitter is may be a problem. Friends, or sitters who are not well recommended, may be too busy to come by on a regular basis, and the dog may be at risk because if there is something wrong, it may go undetected. And dogs may slip past a stranger and leave the area. Just because a dog comes to his master's call does not mean that he will return when called by a stranger even if the stranger knows his name. Many breeders recommended that you try it before you leave. Be sure your Cocker knows the caregiver and will let them into the house and yard in the absence of the family.

One of the great advantages of owning a Cocker Spaniel is that they are small enough to travel with their master. They generally love to go places. Their naturally inquisitive nature makes every trip an adventure. They are hearty and hardy dogs for their size, and love the outdoors. They fit easily into a car without your having to make a decision on whether to take the dog or other members of the family. The American Cocker Spaniel is a good choice for the owner who wants a pal to tag along with him or her.

TRAINING

*E*arly training is very important. A puppy's early training begins with his mother. She teaches him early "law and order," as one breeder put it. When a pup gets too far out of line, she will nip at him, or roll him over on his back. This is a submissive position for a dog and it will make the puppy back down. Pups will also acquire some of their training and socialization from other puppies in the litter. How they relate to each other and the social relationships they develop will be reflected in their personality later in life and the way they relate to other dogs. In the early stage of the puppy's life the breeder will also help in the socialization process. When the ears and eyes open, the puppy needs to develop a relationship with a human, to experience the touch, voice and sight of a human, to develop confidence in humans as caregivers.

When the pup comes home, don't become another pup to him. Nipping, barking and snapping at you may be cute in a puppy, but it will be obnoxious in an adult dog. Don't let his play get out of hand. Cockers can be willful. Never let him on the couch unless you want to share it with him forever. Correct such things as jumping when it is still easy to stop him and it will not develop into a problem.

Housetraining may be the first area where the Cocker may not take the same kind of enthusiastic interest as his owner. One of our breeders suggested tying a bell to the door where the pup is let in and out of the house to play and go to the bathroom. Pups are inquisitive. Ring the bell, then open the door to let the pup out. Soon the natural curiosity of the pup will cause him to nose the bell. When he does, let him out. In this way the pup or older dog learns to ring the bell to go out rather than scratch the door or bark. And

because it is a game, the dog housetrains faster than with normal methods. The advantage is that the dog is trained rather than the owner. (This happens when an owner simply keeps a constant eye on the dog and lets it out every time he thinks the dog needs to use the bathroom.)

The secret to housetraining is consistent training and keeping the dog confined. The more freedom the puppy has, the more likely he is to have an accident. Keep a good watch on the pup when he is not in the crate. Let him play with the family and run through the kitchen only when you are available to watch him. NEVER GIVE A YOUNG PUPPY FREE RUN OF THE HOUSE. Once he gets used to running through the house and having accidents in other rooms, it will be almost impossible to keep him from continuing the habit into adulthood.

One of the biggest problems in housetraining begins when an accident occurs. Once a pup has soiled carpet, or flooring, he will often do so again and again in the same place. This is because urine which dries begins to bond to the carpet fibers. The protein chains of amino acids which make up urine crystallize into salts, forming ionic (electric charge) bonds. Cleaning products cannot break those bonds and the decay of the proteins and the associated bacteria continues to give off an odor which the dog can smell, even when cleaning products have masked the odor to the human inhabitants. The dog smells the area, associates it with elimination, and repeats the offense.

To eliminate the cause of the odor, and therefore the problem which encourages the dog to repeat his mistake, a bacterial/enzyme product must be used. These products actually break down and eliminate the protein chains and the bacterial decay which causes the odor. The technical aspects are too complicated to mention here, but these products are safe and natural and eliminate the problem instead of masking the odor. One such product is *Anti-icky-Poo,* listed in our Shopping Arcade section. This product is excellent and the informational material the manufacturer can provide you will answer the technical questions you might have on the problem. It is important to be aware of this "hidden odor" since replacing carpet and pad without treating the flooring underneath, which may have also been exposed to urine, will only cause the dog to smell the area and continue to use the same spot, soiling the new carpet and continuing the problem.

Use a crate when you are not home, or when you are home and cannot watch him. Let him directly outside when you take him out of the crate, and let him have time to exercise and go to the bathroom and have five to ten minutes of exercise. This will also help his attitude when he comes inside as he will have had a chance to "blow off" some of his energy. Let him outside after eating or drinking, and let him out just before you crate him. This helps establish a pattern of behavior which will encourage housetraining. Remember, young pups need to urinate every forty-five to sixty minutes, and about twenty minutes after drinking water. Bowel movements tend to occur up to five or six times per day, usually about a half an hour after meals and just after waking up in the morning.

Start training pups as early as three months, though it may be four to five months of age before he can make it through the night without a problem. Cockers are ready to learn from an early age, and it is important to get an early start with them. Don't correct the puppy unless he understands why he is being corrected. When teaching him something new, always teach him first until he understands what is expected of him. Only set reasonable goals that the puppy can handle while he is still happy. A puppy's tail is a good barometer. A low tail indicates low spirits so try to keep the spirits and the tail wagging.

If you have a dog already, be aware that your older dog may dominate your new puppy. Do not allow your new puppy to be kenneled or fed with an older dog. The puppy could be permanently ruined by a strong-willed dog. No matter how kind the older dog may seem, he may dominate the younger dog.

The key to early training is positive reinforcement. Always encourage, teach and reward. Shape the behavior with food rewards or verbal encouragement in a way that the puppy understands for maximum psychological development. A puppy that is forced young often remains full of resentment and may lack confidence and poise. Remember, positive mental attitude is promoted with positive reinforcement.

Don't make training sessions too long. The time to quit is before the puppy shows signs of being tired. By keeping the lessons short, you will instill that desire to keep going that all good companion Cockers need. When you work a dog until he refuses, you only teach him to quit whenever he feels like it. Prevent the problem from ever developing by motivating a young puppy to keep going and keep trying.

Aggressive behavior toward other dogs needs to be discouraged early. Care should be taken to avoid excessively aggressive lines. A dog with less than a solid temperament should not be bred, regardless of how fine other qualities may be. Never let your pup show aggressive behavior toward other dogs or animals. Use the word "No." If the problem persists, pick the pup up, look him straight in the eye, and shake him sharply. This is consistent with the behavior of the dam, and in dog language requires submissive behavior, therefore eliminating the aggressive tendencies he is showing.

Leash training should be started early and done firmly. Don't pull a puppy, as you may damage neck muscles. Begin by putting on the leash and following the pup, gently tugging at him to follow you whenever possible. If he pulls back, stand firm. Do not give in to him, but let him fight it out himself. Cockers are easy to leash train and after only a few short lessons you should be able to take him anywhere you want to go.

If started early, Cockers do not mind a regular bath. It is important to start early and be regular about baths and nails. Be firm about not letting him jump out of the bathtub or pull back from the nail trimming. You may need a second person to help hold him, especially as he gets a little older. NEVER GET INTO A FIGHT WITH A PUPPY AND LET HIM WIN or the next time will be more difficult. If you are having trouble with nails, for example, reduce the job to something you can both manage without getting into a fight. Trim one nail a day, or trim off only a small amount that you can manage before he gets too upset.

You will also need to begin early to get him used to a brush and even a blow dryer after a bath. The puppy coat is short, thin and dries easily, but the adult coat will take hours to dry unless it is clipped quite short. Begin to use a hand blow dryer on the pup but be careful it is not set on the hottest setting and does not burn the skin. Do not let the airflow stay in one place too long, or get in the eyes. Eyes will dry out and begin to sting if the dryer flow hits them. Keep the dryer nozzle at a comfortable distance. If the pup tries to bite or play with the brush or dryer, say "No" sharply. You may even need to tap him lightly on the nose. Keep grooming sessions short so that the pup does not get tired.

If you do not intend to do the clipping yourself, most of our breeders recommend picking a grooming salon and beginning to send the pup before he is a year old. This will get him used to the routine of the grooming salon and the same groomer working on him.

Be careful if your puppy seems to be shy of people; he may need more socialization. Socialization and early obedience classes are very helpful in raising a well-adjusted dog. If you intend to show in conformation, local match shows are a wonderful experience for pups and novice handlers. They are small and most people are very friendly and helpful.

Teach your puppy early the meaning of the word "No." When he does something you do not want him to do, tap him on the nose sharply and say "No" firmly. Cockers are smart and there is no reason why you should ever hit your dog. A light smack under the chin was recommended by some of our breeders if there is a persistent problem. A newspaper slapped against the floor, which makes a loud noise, is often a helpful alternative to get a pup's attention.

Cockers are naturally curious and want to explore everything. Not only does this make housetraining difficult, but they are creative enough to get into trouble even in situations which look safe to you. Things you may not notice, such as electric and phone cords, cupboards which open easily, and plants on tables, may be hazards to your Cocker. It is safer to crate your dog than to try to make the house completely puppy safe.

Crate training is useful for traveling and for a variety of different occasions at home. Once adapted to a crate, most dogs like them, and look at them as a secure home. However, the first time or two in a crate may be a problem. Cockers like to bark and if they think they have a reason, they may be quite vocal about the crate at first. When this occurs, whether during crate training or other times when they may be locked in a room or area of the house, a slap on the crate or door with

Decide BEFORE you get your Cocker if he will be allowed on the furniture or you may find he will make his own decisions about where to sleep.

a newspaper and a loud "No" are useful. If the problem persists, a water gun filled with water can be shot at the dog, along with the word "No." The sudden shot of water enforces the word, and is very effective. If nothing else, the reaction will be to distract the puppy from his behavior and get him concentrating on where the water came from rather than on his specific behavior. This is also an effective technique to stop unwanted behavior such as digging, chewing or climbing.

FIELD, AGILITY AND OBEDIENCE TRAINING

One of the reasons we suggest that you decide ahead of time what you want to do with the dog, is that often training should begin at an early age. Field training is an example. Although many feel that the Cocker is no longer suitable for work in the field, a number of people are doing very well with them in just that area of endeavor. One breeder suggested that the Cocker is still very good at field work, but needs a good "Wake up call," to bring out the basic instincts. You can begin a young puppy very early, as young as eight to twelve weeks of age. Begin with a few retrieves and a bird wing or knotted handkerchief with a pheasant scent. And don't scold a puppy for carrying shoes, socks, gloves and other household items or he will learn to hide his retrieved "booty" in a place where he can destroy it in peace. Remember, this is just his retrieving instinct coming to the fore. Praise him, take the item from him, and then put it out of his reach. Don't let him chew up objects, or play tug of war with him. Too easily you will find him chewing up your bird, or find yourself in a tug of war to get the bird he has just retrieved.

Obedience classes can begin at about six months of age. Any time after you have taught him to walk easily on a leash, and have practiced enough so that both of you are comfortable, you can begin to take him to "puppy classes." These classes are offered in most areas and provide socialization and early training for pups. If you are interested in agility, you must first teach him to work off lead, which is an advanced level of obedience training. Remember to always keep training sessions short, and don't expect too much perfection from your Cocker until he is old enough to be mature. Cockers do not concentrate on the task at hand unless they have developed some discipline and this may simply take waiting until he is old enough to pay attention to what is being asked of him. Make the training fun and you will get more enthusiasm and cooperation from your Cocker than if you try to be serious and forceful.

With any of these activities, be prepared to work with your dog on a daily basis and to continue for many months before you are ready for even the most basic level of competition. But you may find that your Cocker is surprisingly good in the field, in the obedience ring or on the agility course.

BREEDING YOUR DOG -
WHY THIS MIGHT NOT BE SUCH A GOOD IDEA!

Now that you have your dog, you may entertain the idea that you should breed it. If you read one of the larger books on the breed or one of the many dog books that discusses breeding, they discuss genetics, how to build a whelping box, and they make it sound easy. The breeders and breed associations will say that you "should not breed your dog." That makes it sound like an ethical decision on a high moral plane, and you may be tempted to simply say, "But I just want one litter; what could it hurt?" Here is probably the most honest evaluation of why this may be one of the many times in life when something LOOKS better on the outside than it does when you actually TRY it.

Have you ever gone somewhere and seen a WONDERFUL layout of model trains or a large doll house? The hobby looked easy and fascinating. You may have even gone home and bought a small doll house kit, or a starter set of trains. Then you began to discover just how much time and money really went into this simple looking project. You needed space to work on the project, and space to set it up. You needed special tools and materials you had never worked with before, and they were all expensive. You had to spend time shopping for the right pieces of the right size so that it all went together. The pieces that went into it were expensive. Very quickly you found that this seemingly simple set-up was going to cost you hours and hours of your life and hundreds of dollars just to get off to a good start. And when you put together the first pieces, it was a boring, poor substitute for the intricate, fascinating set-up you had seen. In the end, you gave up on it, losing the money you HAD invested in the train set which is now on a shelf in the garage, or the dollhouse which still sits without those hundreds of maddening little shingles pasted to the roof! In short, your time and money was not well spent unless you found it to be something you were interested in to the point where you became involved and dedicated!

Like all hobbies, there is much more to dog breeding than first meets the eye. Enthusiasts put time and money into this, just as with any hobby. The result which looks

simple is the product of careful planning and investment. To do it in any way short of that kind of planning will result in something far short of the goal, which is a waste of your time and money. Even a single litter can consume much more time and money than you ever imagined on the way into the project.

In 1994, over 22,689 litters of American Cocker Spaniels were registered with AKC. This is up from 1993, when over 22,562 litters were registered. But the most interesting thing is that the number of individual animals being registered numbered 60,888, down from 1993 figures of 75,882. This means that although the number of litters in 1994 went up, people were not bothering to register their dogs. Every year there are thousands of puppies which do not even show up in the statistics, all bearing some resemblance to a Cocker Spaniel, and flooding the market with poor quality pups. If an owner does not care enough about his dog or think it is important to register the dog in the first place, common sense says that he will not put much care into the planning of the breeding if he decides to

have a litter. While he may take care of the bitch, he will not be well educated in how to socialize the pups in their early development, how to select a puppy which will fit your home, or how to predict which health problems may occur! This also means that should you decide to produce a litter without proper dedication to the sport, you will be competing for the bottom end homes for your puppies with this very flooded market. With that kind of population, it is no wonder that the breed has suffered in quality, health and temperament. All American Cocker Spaniels are simply NOT alike!!

Most people decide to breed their dog for one of the following reasons::

A) It looks like easy money. Call a few breeders, find out the price of pups, and the number of pups in a litter, and the profit doesn't look bad. But remember, you are playing the Kibbles and Bits Slot Machine. You may make money on a litter here and there, but there is a greater potential to lose money, sanity, friends and routine. The odds are better at Las Vegas. How much stress is it worth to you to make a few dollars? How many nice things are in your home that you would prefer not to see with tooth marks? And like any new business venture, there is ALWAYS investment before there is profit. How much are you willing to invest before you have a pay-off?

B) People think that it would be a wonderful experience for the children. But the kids will play with the pups for a few days and then go back to Nintendo or outside to play ball, depending on what their interests are. A litter of eight-week-old pups is too young to have manners enough to stay away from Nintendo controls, but too small to play with the kids! In the end, the kids may find the pups more annoying than interesting. It is like having four or five toddlers around the house. One of our breeders remembers several times when her children took the pups out of the puppy area, then got interested in something else, forgot about the pups, and left unhousetrained pups prying into every corner of the house unsupervised! If you want the kids to see the joy of birth, BUY A VIDEO. It's cheaper, more informative, and in the end the house smells better!

C) You may decide you want a second dog. Friends and family have said they also wanted a dog. But frequently friends who have repeatedly said, "If you ever breed Fluffy, we want a pup," will be the first to tell you AFTER the litter is eight weeks old and you have asked them when they are going to get their puppy, that they "really can't take a puppy this time, but for sure the next time you breed her!" Besides, most of these people will want a puppy for free, and why should you invest time and money just to get them a free dog?

D) There may be no decision at all. A neighborhood male jumped the fence. (Yes, even six footers have been known to be scaled.) The bitch slipped out past the kids when she was in season. No one realized that she was in season. The list goes on and on. It is much easier to get an accidental breeding than you can ever imagine. Mixed litters are the hardest to get rid of, and you have all the disadvantages of raising a litter with none of the advantage of producing a nice puppy, or being able to sell it. For this reason, we highly recommend that you SPAY ANY BITCH YOU DID NOT BUY FOR THE EXPRESS PURPOSE OF BREEDING OR SHOWING.

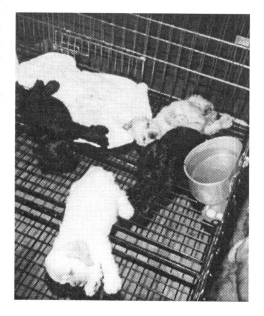

If you bought your dog as a pet, you may find that you have a limited registration, which means that your pups are not eligible for registration. The breeder, with his knowledge of the gene pool for the breed in general and his line in particular, may have priced your dog as a pet and found a pet home for her because for some reason he did not feel that puppies should be produced from her.

When you consider breeding your dog, think about some very important factors.

First, did you buy a nice quality dog from a good breeder? Is this a dog the breeder himself would want to breed? If the answer is "NO," don't breed your dog just to get a litter of puppies. It is this kind of breeding that lowers the quality of the Cocker Spaniel and gives the breed a bad name. If you did not make it clear that you were looking for a breeding bitch at the time of purchase, the chances are that your bitch is not of breeding quality. This goes back to the necessity of making it very clear *what* you want the dog for at the time of purchase. There may be hidden genetic problems that the breeder knows are in your dog — ones that will not affect her life and health, but which may appear in her puppies. The breeder may not have explained this to you because you said all you wanted was a pet. As long as *your* dog was not affected by it, there was no reason for the breeder to go into it. But if you breed the dog, it will surely appear again and then *you* are the breeder who has to deal with the problem. Then *you* will have puppy buyers coming back to you with a problem with your puppies. How will you handle it?

Second, even though there are a lot of dogs in the newspaper every week, remember that with all of the Cockers out there, it may not be as easy as it looks to sell the pups. It is one thing to look at a litter of five pups and say to yourself, "Even at $200 each, that is $1,000!" and another to reap that kind of profit. The road is filled with pitfalls, chewed furniture, expenses that add up like a city street repair budget, and more work than coaching a Little League team!

It may sound like a jackpot. You appear to do nothing and extra pocket money comes rolling in! But think about the expenses you incur. Pups need shots and worming. Even if your vet is very reasonable, $50 is the lowest you will pay ($25 for the office call and $5 per pup).

You have the expense of the puppy food and the additional food the bitch will require during the time she is carrying and nursing. You have to build or buy a box for her to have them in or she will pick the bed, a closet (after she has pulled all of the clothes off the hangers to make her own bed) or the middle of the flower bed.

Advertising in the local newspaper will run $20 to $40 per weekend. Count the number of Cocker ads in your newspaper. The odds are that you will not be able to sell the entire litter in one weekend. It

will take you two or three *at best*. You will have to stay home to answer the phone, and you will have at least a dozen strangers coming to your home to see the pups, and many of them will simply be on an outing. Cockers are cute pups and there are the inevitable "window shoppers." The price of one to two pups will be needed JUST TO COVER THE EXPENSE YOU HAVE IN RAISING THE LITTER AND SELLING IT.

And here are some other things that can go wrong: there is the expense and trouble of the breeding. Either one pup or a stud fee is usually paid to the owner of the stud, even if he is a local dog. Stud fees on known dogs run around $500 and many breeders will ask that the fee be paid at the time the breeding is made. This is six to eight weeks before the litter is born, and about four months before you can sell the pups. If you have picked a dog from some distance away, you will need to ship either the bitch or the semen. Shipping the frozen semen is easier, but then you must pay a vet, or someone who is authorized to make the breeding, to inseminate the bitch.

If you are breeding to a good stud, you will have to plan ahead to book the breeding. It is best to start that *before* the bitch comes in season. You will need to send a copy of your bitch's pedigree and perhaps her picture to the owner of the stud for approval in most cases. When it is time for breeding, you will have to get a current brucellosis test. Although uncommon, brucellosis is a contagious disease which is usually sexually transmitted between dogs. It can be contagious to humans from handling the dogs during breeding or whelping, and there is some new evidence to show that it can also be transmitted between dogs through waste material. Rather than risk it, most breeders will require a current brucellosis certificate. A test from six months or a year before is not considered current. Many breeders will also require hip and eye certification.

Bitches shed after they have a litter. Do not expect them to be in top condition for several months. Many Cocker bitches will lose part or most of their hair after whelping.

There are often problems with a sale. Someone buys a pup and it gets sick, and they want YOU to pay the vet bill. Or they can't keep it and want to bring it back. Someone brings in a virus and the litter gets sick and you have hundreds of dollars of vet bills — it happens all the time. Even the best breeders have problems with a virus in a litter from time to time.

As the pups begin to move around, they may get out of their area and chew up furniture or kitchen cabinets. The force of a litter of wiggling, happy, uncontrollable seven-week-old puppies is enough to move such things as baby gates and temporary pens, and scratch up back doors. Outside, these little fellows will dig and chew up bushes unless you have a specific pen built for them. Now we are into the expense of building some place to contain them between the time the bitch has had enough, and you can sell them. This could be the longest month of your life!

And winter puppies, inside because of the cold weather, will shred papers, take down barriers, and create literally several pounds of wet and soiled papers a day. Mopping and scraping smeared puppy poop will become a way of life! Certainly there are crates and cages called "puppy play pens" which do a very good job containing puppies and eliminating some of the mess. But they will run in the neighborhood of $140 each and will take up a

space of about 4' X 4' in some inconvenient place in your home!

In short, many people breed a litter because they think it is easy money, they want the "experience" of having a litter (which is a little like wanting to have the "experience of juggling five bowling balls without dropping them on your foot!) and because they want the kids to have the fun of a litter. They may want a second dog and this looks like a way to get one for themselves, friends or family members.

By the time you add up expenses, it is cheaper to simply buy a nice second dog. One puppy is fun, two are a chore and four can be overwhelming if you are not set up for it and if you do not have the time to devote to it. Breeders do this as a hobby. It interests them, they have invested time and money — just as you would with any hobby that interests you — in finding the best way to handle pups. Every one of them has early disaster stories to tell.

And perhaps this is the time to mention that the odor of your home may change, and friends may be less inclined to visit. Whelping has a distinctive smell. Amniotic fluid is dark green, stains what it comes in contact with, and has a permeating fragrance. Although the bitch will clean up after the litter when they are very young, her housekeeping may be somewhat lax when they get older and start on solid food. One of our breeders said she bought a breadmaking machine so that the aroma of yeast and fresh bread would fill the house instead of the aroma of puppies!

Time is another thing you will need. Are you prepared to stay home when the bitch is ready to whelp? In accordance with Murphy's Law, the bitch is guaranteed to whelp in the middle of a dinner party, or on the day you have an important appointment — even if she has to be days early or days late to do it! The need for a Caesarean section can lead to even more time and expense. First time bitches are often poor or confused mothers who do not clean pups well, or who step on pups. You should always be present at a whelping, especially of a first time bitch, or risk losing pups and/or the dam. And there are a tremendous number of health issues which may arise. These may threaten both the bitch and pups. It can lead to vet expenses which can overwhelm you.

After they are born, you will need to start handling the pups from the beginning. Watch for poor nursers. Sometimes you will need to physically put a puppy which is nursing slowly, or who is getting shoved out of a big litter, on the tit and hold him on until he can get his fill. There is always the chance that one or more of the pups will need tube or bottle feeding at least as a supplement. There is the time you will need to take them to the vets for shots, and the time you will need to spend with them just getting them used to people and being handled. And there is the inevitable clean-up time. When the litter gets older, they will be glad to try to help you with these chores by eating the mop, broom or papers as you are trying to get the job done. This kind of help does not speed up the process. Pups need to be fed and cared for like babies, in the morning when you are late, and at night when you are tired.

One of our breeders said, "The amazing thing about it is that when a mother sheep has baby sheep, the mother sheep takes care of them. When a mother horse has a baby horse, the mother horse takes care of it. But when a bitch whelps, YOU take care of them!"

If you truly are interested in breeding dogs, go to some shows, talk to breeders, do your homework for the next phase of your hobby, just as we have advised you throughout this book. Determine the style of dog you want to breed, the temperament you feel a Cocker should have, and the purpose you want your puppies to fill in their new homes. Consider that you will need to keep several pups from your first litters in order to see how well your breeding program is working. Do you have room for several adults?

Then, study the pedigrees to find out what bloodlines are most likely to produce the type of dog you want. Decide how you will determine if you are reaching your goal. Will you show them to check their conformation quality? Will you temperament test them, check on the pups after they have been placed in homes, use them as therapy dogs? What kind of homes will they fit into, and how will you sell them? What kind of guarantee will you offer new owners? How will you handle problems which may arise with new owners who are having a problem with their puppies? Do you have enough experience to be able to help them, or can you get the information from a mentor breeder?

From a practical standpoint, how will you handle the litter? Look at facilities of other breeders. Ask what kinds of equipment you will need. Ask about vaccinations and eye care. Find a good vet who is familiar with the breed and the eye problems. Do you have a vet who knows anything about whelping and caring for a litter? Where will you get help if something goes wrong? Do you have the time to socialize them, and a clear idea of how you will do it?

We strongly advise finding a breeder who is willing to work with you as a mentor. They have the experience you will need to tap into and can give you advice along the way if things don't go as planned.

After you have thought out the project completely, do your first breeding. Like anything else, careful planning and forethought can save stress, money, grief and your home!

Some of our breeders recounted how they got started. For many, it was a matter of seeing a dog they liked, investigating his lines, and finding the right person to help and advise them. Then they invested as much money as they could afford in the best bitch they could find. Sometimes this worked, but many of our breeders reported starting again and again until they got the right foundation stock, clear of problems and representing the ideal they had in mind for the breed. Some of the best advice came from an old breeder who said, "Never get attached to a breeding bitch." If you have a pet, and she turns out to be a poor producer (and even top winners may not be good producers or good mothers), keep her, love her, BUT STOP BREEDING HER! If you wish to continue breeding, purchase another bitch.

There is a lot more to breeding than owning a pet. If you intend to do it, be sure that you do it as well as you can. This will provide you with the best possible chance of producing quality puppies and having happy new owners.

SHOPPING ARCADE

THE FOLLOWING SECTION IS A SHOWCASE OF FINE COMPANIES WHO PRODUCE AND SELL PRODUCTS WHICH ARE OF INTEREST TO AMERICAN COCKER SPANIEL OWNERS.

Many of these goods and services you will not find in the course of your normal shopping patterns. Those who are involved with dogs and dog shows are used to finding an abundance of these kinds of products at the many show vendors they see each weekend, but we know that many of our readers do not have the same opportunity. We hope that by presenting these companies to you here, it will make your life with your American Cocker Spaniel a little richer and easier. Please feel free to write us and let us know how you feel about this section, or this book in general. We encourage your comments and would like to hear from you. If at any time after publication you cannot make contact with a company listed in this section, or a breeder listed in the breeder sections, please contact Dace Publishing to get an updated number.

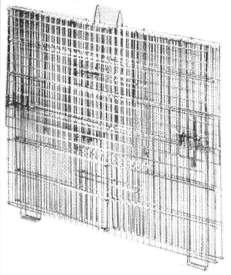
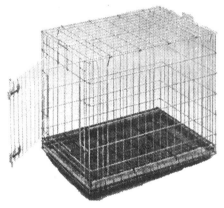

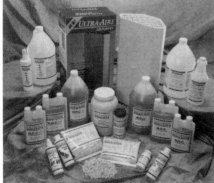

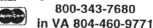

ANIMAL ART CONTEST

Any Media - Any breed of dog or type of pet.

*Cash Prizes   *Gift Certificates *Publication

Division I - Adults   Division II - Jr. - under 20 yrs.

Bi-annual contest - Prizes awarded in each contest!

NO LIMIT TO THE NUMBER OF ENTRIES,
OR THE NUMBER OF SUCCESSIVE CONTESTS.

ENTRY DEADLINES: March 30 and Sept. 30

Entry FEE: $15.00 per entry,   *Entry fee must accompany entry.*

Send: Artwork ; name, address and phone number with entry fee. State age if under 20

Mail to: Dace, P.O. Box 91, Ruckersville VA 22968

ART CONTEST WINNER

This excellent pen and ink is by Dave Brown of Virginia.

PHOTO CONTEST WINNER

This lovely photo of young American Cocker Spaniels was submitted by Evelyn P. Bravo, of Chantrel Cocker Spaniels.

CH. DAZLIN MYSTIC COMMAND

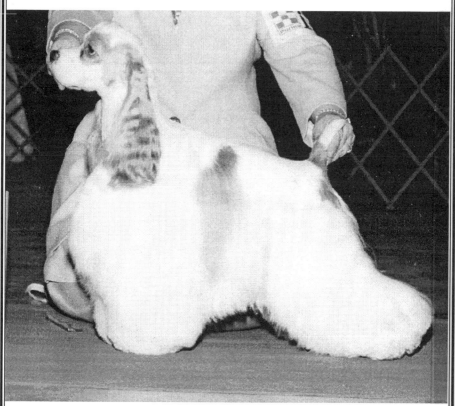

Ch. Dazlin's Mystic Command

Ch. Shalimar's In Command
- Ch. Terje's Thunderbolt
  - Ch. Dal Mar's Billy Jack
  - Ch. Swank's Short N Sweet
- Ch. Shalimar's Soft Touch
  - Ch. Andmor's Double Distinctive
  - Ch. Shalimar's Devastation

B Sky's Mystic Sara
- Ch. Gloriland's Jeremiah
  - Ch. Legend Dudley DoRight
  - Ch. Bonny Jay's Hosanna
- B Sky's Mystic Danielle
  - Ch. Southwind Shikari
  - Chi Lee's Sky Crickette

LP is champion 6 of the 8 we've produced by crossing B-Sky's Mystic Sara to the Shalimar dogs (brothers Perry - aka Imperator, and Larry - aka In Command). Never specialed, LP finished with multiple majors and Best of Variety wins over some of the nations top-ranked Specials. He is typical of the tall, elegant-moving, sound dogs that came from our "first generation". Although young yet, the off-spring of these dogs and bitches from Perry and Sara are showing m u c h promise for the future!

Becki and Dale Zaborowski
6732 Romain Dr
Acworth, GA 30102-1151
(404) 974-7931

DAZLIN

National Institute on Alcohol Abuse and Alcoholism

R  ÑOGRAPH - 30

Alcohol and Tobacco: From Basic Science to Clinical Practice

U.S. DEPARTMENT OF HEALTH AND HUMAN SERVICES
Public Health Service
National Institutes of Health